TWAYNE'S WORLD AUTHORS SERIES

A Survey of the World's Literature

Sylvia E. Bowman, Indiana University
GENERAL EDITOR

SPAIN

Gerald E. Wade, Vanderbilt University
EDITOR

Juan Goytisolo

(*TWAS* 104)

TWAYNE'S WORLD AUTHORS SERIES (TWAS)

The purpose of TWAS is to survey the major writers —novelists, dramatists, historians, poets, philosophers, and critics—of the nations of the world. Among the national literatures covered are those of Australia, Canada, China, Eastern Europe, France, Germany, Greece, India, Italy, Japan, Latin America, New Zealand, Poland, Russia, Scandinavia, Spain, and the Latin Classical literatures. This survey is complemented by Twayne's United States Authors Series and English Authors Series.

The intent of each volume in these series is to present a critical-analytical study of the works of the writer; to include biographical and historical material that may be necessary for understanding, appreciation, and critical appraisal of the writer; and to present all material in clear, concise English—but not to vitiate the scholarly content of the work by doing so.

Juan Goytisolo

photo: Lutfi Ozkok, Sweden

JUAN GOYTISOLO

Preface

O F the older writers who discuss contemporary Spain, only
Ramón Sender (b. 1902), who was famous before the Spanish
Civil War, and Camilo José Cela (b. 1916), the initiator of the
so-called *tremendista* vogue of the 1940's, have achieved a world-
wide reputation. Among the more than two hundred novelists
who wrote after the Civil War, largely reflecting their anguish
and despair brought about directly or indirectly by that tragic
conflict, some like Rafael Sánchez Ferlosio, Ana María Matute,
and Miguel Delibes have achieved a reputation for excellence.
Among the younger writers, Juan Goytisolo has perhaps received
the most critical attention and is, in the opinion of many, the
leading exponent of the new novel in Spain.

Goytisolo combines the traditional picaresque social novel,
which originated in Spain, with modern reportorial, temporal,
cinematographic, semi-objectivist, and stylistic innovations, to
treat the post-war generations and their problems, especially
those of children and young adults. Among his admitted influences are Pío Baroja, Valle-Inclán, Truman Capote, Carson
McCullers, and William Faulkner.

The aim of this book is to explain historical, stylistic, philosophical, and cultural forces, inherited and refashioned by Goytisolo, to show how he used them for social causes and esthetic
concerns, and to attempt to fix his place in twentieth-century
Spanish literature.

JUAN GOYTISOLO

by

KESSEL SCHWARTZ

The aim of this book is to present the stylistic, philosophical, historical, and cultural forces which Goytisolo inherited and which he refashioned. An examination of each of his works reveals how he used these forces and enables one to arrive at an over-all appreciation of Goytisolo's position among contemporary Spanish novelists.

The post-Civil War period in Spain largely reflected the anguish and despair caused by that tragic conflict, but it brought forth few fresh and internationally known novelists, in spite of the several hundred writers who have produced novels in this period. With the exception of Ramón Sender, who was known before the Civil War, and Camilo José Cela, the originator of *tremendista* works in the 1940's, Juan Goytisolo is the author who has received more critical attention than any other Spanish novelist in the 1950's and 1960's.

Goytisolo combines the traditional picaresque social novel, originating in Spain, with modern reportorial, cinematographic, and stylistic innovations as he treats the post-war generations and their problems.

ABOUT THE AUTHOR

. Kessel Schwartz was born in Kansas City, Missouri, on March 19, 1920. He obtained the B.A. Degree with Distinction in Spanish from the University of Missouri in 1940, the M.A. in 1941, and the Ph.D. from Columbia University in New York in 1953. He has taught at Hamilton College, the University of Vermont, the University of Arkansas, where he was Chairman of the Department of Romance Languages, and at the University of Miami at Coral Gables, where he was also Chairman of the Department until 1964. He continues there as Professor of Spanish Language and Literature on the Graduate Faculty. During 1946-48 he was Director of Cultural Centers in Nicaragua and Ecuador.

Dr. Schwartz is the author of six books, including *A New History of Spanish Literature* (with Richard Chandler), 1961, and *Introduction to Modern Spanish Literature,* Twayne Publishers, 1967. He has written some thirty-five articles and a dozen reviews in a variety of scholarly journals such as *Hispania, Revista Hispanica Moderna, Symposium, Revista Iberoamericana, Romance Notes, Modern Drama, Journal of Inter-American Studies,* and *Hispanic American Historical Review.* His two fields of specialization are Modern Spanish Literature and Latin American Literature, with special emphasis on the novel. He has edited a text on Juan Goytisolo and has written articles on that author.

Dr. Schwartz is a member of Sigma Delta Pi, Phi Sigma Iota, Phi Beta Kappa, and is listed in *Who's Who in the South and Southwest, Who's Who in American Education, Who's Who in America, Dictionary of American Scholars, Contemporary Authors, International Platform Association,* and *Honorarium Americana.* During 1964 he was Secretary of Group 5, Modern Spanish Literature, of the Modern Language Association, and in 1965 was Chairman of Group 5. He was a nominating committee member for the Twentieth-Century Literature Section of the Modern Language Association, 1966-1968. For 1966-1968 he was also Associate Editor of *Hispania.*

Contents

Chronology

1931   January 5: Juan Goytisolo Gay born at Barcelona, the birthplace also of his parents, of Spanish, Basque, and French ancestry.

1936-   During the Spanish Civil War, lived in small village in the
1939   Republican Zone in Catalonia.

1938   Mother died in Franco bombardment.

1939   Spent summer in country house owned by his father near Barcelona, the scene of *Duelo en el Paraíso* (*Sorrow at Paradise House*). The house is used as a school for orphan children.

1942   Composed a novel about Joan of Arc. Early literary ability was not unusual in his family. His maternal great uncle was a poet; his brother, José Agustín, a poet; and Luis, his other brother, a short story writer and novelist.

1946   Wrote a cowboy novel, never published.

1949   Finished his Bachillerato (high school and junior college) at a Jesuit school.

1950-   Studied law at the University of Barcelona and at the
1951   University of Madrid.

1951   Founded the "Turia" literary group with the novelist Ana María Matute and others in Barcelona. Wrote his first short stories, "El ladrón" ("The Thief") and "El perro asirio" ("The Assyrian Dog").

1952   Won Joven Literatura (Young Literature) Prize, founded by the editor Janes, for his short story, "El mundo de los espejos" ("The World of Mirrors"), but the censor refused to allow its publication. Goytisolo also wrote a novelette, *El soldadito* (*The Little Soldier*).

1952   Wrote *Juegos de manos* (*Sleight of Hand*).

1953   Received law degree at the University of Barcelona.

1954   *Juegos de manos* published. Visits Paris.

1955   *Duelo en el Paraíso* published. Wins the *Indice* Prize. Wrote *Fiestas*.

1957   Went to live in Paris and to work for the Gallimard Publishing House.

1957   *El circo (The Circus)* published.

1958   *La resaca (The Undertow)* published.

1958   *Duelo en el Paraíso* translated into English as *Children of Chaos.*

1958   *Fiestas* published.

1959   *Juegos de manos* translated into English as *The Young Assassins.*

1959   *Problemas de la novela (Problems of the Novel)*, largely based on articles written for the review *Destino* between 1956 and 1958, published.

1960   *Campos de Níjar (Fields of Níjar)* published.

1960   *Para vivir aquí (To Live Here)*, short stories, published.

1961   *La isla (The Island)* published.

1962   *La Chanca* published.

1962   *Fin de fiesta (Holiday's End)*, four novelettes, published.

1963   *Pueblo en marcha (People on the March)* published.

1966   *Señas de identidad (Signs of Identity)* published.

1967   *El furgón de cola* (The Caboose) published.

CHAPTER 1

Historical Background

I *The Civil War, Censorship, and the Economic Situation*

TO UNDERSTAND the background of Goytisolo's novels, the people and situations he examines, the end-of-the-war incidents and the war's aftermath to which he refers, an examination of the war and especially post-Civil War Spain is needed. Goytisolo, peripherally and in flashbacks, often refers to events preceding and during the war of 1936-1939. He deals directly with events occurring during the last days of the war in 1939 and with happenings of the following twenty-five years.

The February, 1936, elections had caused violent outbreaks of fighting between the Right and the Left. Although leaders of the Republic knew that army generals were conspiring to overthrow it, they took inadequate measures to protect themselves and their government. On July 18, implementing the verbal attacks which right-wing leaders had been making in Congress for months, the generals started a revolt against the government. Francisco Franco, a regular army officer, subdued Morocco and established a Fascist government on the mainland at Burgos. As the Civil War grew in violence, destruction, and bloodshed, Italy and Germany lent military and the Pope moral support to Franco. The rebels obtained troops, technicians, weapons, airplanes, and aviators from Germany and Italy, and, in lesser measure, the Republic received help from the Soviet Union and from volunteer sympathizers from many parts of the world. Franco's superior forces caused the Republicans (the Loyalist army) to retreat, and eventually the rebels (the Nationalists) laid siege to Madrid. The Loyalists fought valiantly, as the Republic's seat of government was moved first to Valencia and then to Barcelona. On

April 15, 1938, Franco's forces reached the sea and divided the Republic. Barcelona fell and on February 27, 1939, Britain and France recognized Franco as the head of the Spanish government. President Azaña escaped to France. Finally, on March 28, 1939, Franco's troops entered Madrid. The new government took terrible reprisals for real and imagined crimes, killing many and imprisoning others who had opposed Franco's rebellion.

During the Second World War Spain remained technically neutral, but volunteer troops from Spain, the Blue Division, fought beside the Germans on the Russian front, and Spain contributed raw materials to the German cause. In 1947, Franco announced that Spain was a kingdom, but the Spanish National Congress named him Chief of State for life with the right to appoint his successor. Spain was excluded from Marshall Plan aid, and Franco was unsuccessful in securing loans. Yet the Civil War in which a million Spaniards had died and the acute economic difficulties depressed the Spanish spirit and made immediate political upheavals a remote possibility. In 1951, the United States sent an ambassador to Madrid, and Franco made several cabinet changes which to some indicated a liberalizing policy. The United States also made loans to Spain to speed her economic recovery. In 1952 Spain became a member of the United Nations Educational, Scientific and Cultural Organization. In 1953 Spain and the United States signed a treaty which allowed the latter country to have military bases on Spanish soil in return for approximately a quarter of a billion dollars in economic and military aid. Spain became a member of the United Nations in 1955.

In 1969 over thirty million Spaniards still lack political freedom, as Franco continues to govern as Commander in Chief of the Armed Forces and Caudillo of Spain. The new generations resent propaganda and what they term obscurantism. They want money, security, and comfort, and blame the bishops, the bankers, and the generals for their difficulties. The university students are afraid of the police; an angry and growing minority among them, indifferent to arrest and imprisonment, are increasingly drawn to socialist, anarchist, and communist ideas.

Goytisolo's generation also blames the Falange, and has often had direct confrontations with its members. Since the Falange plays such a large part in Spanish history of the last thirty years, and since the term is not universally known, a brief description of its development follows. The terms Falangist, Fascist, and Nationalist are often used interchangeably in referring to Franco's followers who took part in what they like to call the "glorious movement" (the July, 1936, revolt). However, the original Falangists were almost all of the upper middle class or the aristocracy. José Antonio Primo de Rivera held the organization's first meeting on October 29, 1933. They accepted the totalitarian ideas of Germany and Italy, emphasizing especially authority and military glory, but they differed philosophically from more orthodox Fascists in rejecting an amalgamation of classes into a national whole. They felt they could achieve a Fascist state without popular support.

On February 11, 1934, the Falange merged with the Juntas de Ofensiva Nacional Sindicalista (Juntas of National Syndicalist Offensive), usually known as JONS. Anti-communistic and virulently anti-Semitic in nature, the JONS had been formed on October 10, 1931 by Ramiro Ledesma Ramos and Onésimo Redondo Ortega. The new organization issued its official proclamation of the formation of the Spanish Falange on March 4, 1934, defending authority and order and attacking liberal traditions. On April 19, 1937, Franco merged the Falange with the ultra right wing Comunión Tradicionalista (Traditionalist Communion), and the new organization became known as the Falange Española Tradicionalista y de las JONS, usually referred to simply as the Falange. Under Franco's control the Falange, among its other activities, became dedicated to the extermination of the Left.

After the war, hunger was prevalent in spite of wheat imports from foreign countries. Republicans were hunted down, jailed, killed, or driven across the Pyrenees. Many former leftists joined the Fascist labor organizations to find jobs and political security, and almost all Spaniards had to try to remake their lives in a land of ruined agriculture and industry. Spain supported the Nazis, and the Falangists hoped for a new place in the sun for Spain through its support of Germany, certain that their chosen heroes could not be defeated. After 1942, when the Nazis began to lose, some monarchists began to oppose Franco, but the latter, with the aid of the Falange, shot thousands of anarchists, liberals, and monarchists, including a great number of students, and imprisoned others. Through the years Franco's shaky, corrupt regime has been bolstered by the United States, due to the latter's desire to maintain its bases, and by his Concordat with the Vatican in 1953.

In 1956 liberal students increased their agitation, and fighting broke out between them and the Falangists. Franco threatened purges and completed University City on the outskirts of Madrid, so that the students might not infect the center of the city with their ideas. Between 1956 and 1959 tremendous inflation almost brought Spain to bankruptcy. Discontented young workers emigrated to West Germany, Switzerland, and France for better jobs at higher pay. By 1962, labor unrest, especially in Asturias, had grown to major proportions. The mine workers constantly rebelled, and many young priests, defying the displeasure of their bishops, aligned themselves with the strikers. Certain elements of the Falange, in an amazing switch, by 1963 were denouncing Spain's capitalism and demanding labor and land reforms.

Many among the older generations, especially the women, support Franco for having "saved Spain from Communism" in the Civil War. The middle class, living well physically, is indifferent to the plight of others and refuses to face possible alternatives. The younger intellectuals and their followers, however, want separation of Church and State, freedom to organize, and the withdrawal of American bases.[1] They resent Franco's paternalistic despotism, but he remains dedicated to his concept of his "glorious Civil War victory." "We did not win the regime we have today hypocritically with some votes," Franco reminded the Spanish nation in September, 1962. "We won it at the point of the bayonet and with the blood of our best people!"[2] These situations are constantly reflected and discussed in Goytisolo's novels.

The Civil War has been the other major influence, the revindication of Spain's *amour propre* . . . the Spanish Army for the first time in half a century had a victory to boast, not a defeat to explain away. A new legend arose: the legend of the holy "crusade" against Communism.

Historical Background

The flower of Spain—the army, the Church, the Carlists, and the Falange—gave Spain rebirth through fire and sword, the legend runs. It was the doctrine of the Inquisition: salvation of the soul by destruction of tainted flesh. So firmly entrenched is this legend now that no army officer would dare challenge it . . . To them, any Spaniard who is not pro Franco is ipso facto a *rojo*, a Red[3]

The earliest historical setting which Goytisolo treats extensively as part of his plot framework occurs in 1939. In *Señas de identidad* (*Signs of Identity*), his latest novel, he returns briefly to 1934 and 1936, and in other novels he comments on even earlier events, but these are largely peripheral to his principal concerns. One of his most persistent references is to the bombing incidents of 1938—his own mother was killed in such a raid. Italian planes bombed small towns and villages unmercifully,

. . . and women and children were mangled in the streets and in their homes. The British commission, investigating on the ground, reported that no military objectives had existed. The purpose was to terrorize and demoralize the civilian population behind the lines and to drive them into Barcelona and Valencia to swell the enormous number of refugees, dependent on a hard-pressed government for food.[4]

The bombs were not aimed at military objectives. They were dropped designedly in the center, the most populous section of the city, where people were dining, walking, sleeping in their beds. When these raids ended, nine hundred men, women and children were mangled corpses, blown in many cases to bits, disemboweled . . . a bus, filled with noncombatants, mostly women and children . . . a moment later another bomb made a clean hit on the bus, and the women and children were mere fragments of human flesh smeared on the pavement.[5]

Censorship in Spain has muzzled and hypnotized its people and driven poets, authors, and artists into exile. As late as 1962 the memberships of golf clubs, dinner lists of more than ten guests, and advertisements had to be approved before publication. This censorship refuted Franco's own Charter, whose Article XII guarantees freedom of speech. No criticism is allowed, and the Civil War has been kept alive. The same generals, bishops, and Falangists make the same speeches over and over, as nothing has really changed. Although officially censorship was removed in 1966, no genuine freedom of thought or expression exists. One may write many things, but one must be willing to suffer the consequences, and almost three decades of imposed conformity have destroyed much of the capacity for an effective intellectual rebellion.

Nevertheless, tourism, moving pictures, and trade pacts opened Spain to new ideas. Pedro Laín Entralgo, rector at the University of Madrid and author of many literary and philosophical studies of Spanish culture, conducted a poll which showed that seventy-five per cent of the students found the government to be incompetent and eighty-five per cent felt the ruling classes were immoral. Fifty-two per cent thought the ecclesiastical hierarchy was "immoral, ostentatious, and ambitious."[6]

II *The Church and Change*

The conservative pressure of the Church appears in all of Goytisolo's novels. The end of the Spanish Civil War signified a return to a more traditional Catholicism, as higher ranking clergy remained indifferent to the problems of social justice and the practical application of charity. The concordat between Franco's government and the Church detailed this return to traditionalism. "With the triumph of the Glorious National Uprising, Spanish legislation has recovered the stamp of her catholicity. Not the catholicity of the nineteenth century, but the catholicity of those who knew how to impose upon it the sign of their greatness—the Catholic Kings and the Imperial Austrian Monarchy."[7] The hierarchy remained largely loyal to Franco. It had a religious monopoly, controlled education, and helped censor books, television, and the theater. In 1957 the Cardinal Primate, fearing "leftist" ideas on social reform among younger priests, ordered a rigid tightening of discipline. The progressives and the traditionalists argue over many Church matters, but the Spanish Church still uses a catechism which lists Darwinism, Deism, Protestantism, Socialism, Liberalism, and Modernism as errors. The Spanish Church continues to denounce any progressive turn of events and is completely opposed to the ecumenical changes proposed by Pope John XXIII in his encyclicals, *Mater et Magistra* (Mother and Teacher) and *Pacem in Terris* (Peace on Earth).

Yet as John Devlin reports in his work on Spanish anticlerical-

ism, *Juventud Obrera* (*Working Youth*), a Catholic workers'
movement which defended strikes (a crime against the nation,
according to the Labor Charter), was

. . . publicly backed by Cardinal Bueno y Monreal, Archbishop of
Seville and successor to Cardinal Segura . . . Freedom of debate and
opinion has been openly upheld in at least two recent legal cases . . .
It was reported on February 26, 1963, that the Bishop of Huelva,
Pedro Cantero Cuadrado, had strongly advocated that current legal
restrictions for non-Catholic religions in Spain be adjusted to conform
more to the "mental and political structure of the European and
Western Community." . . . An absolutely unprecedented attack against
the policies of the present Spanish regime . . . was made by the
Benedictine Abbot of the ancient, venerable Monastery of Montserrat
near Barcelona . . . The eminent Abbot, Dom Aureli M. Escarre, first
charged that "the Spanish government gives a dazzling propaganda
picture of material progress, not progress of liberty and justice . . . We
have not had twenty-five years of peace. We have had twenty-five
years of victory. The victors, including the Church, . . . have done
nothing to close the gap . . . This is one of the most lamentable
failures of a régime that calls itself Christian, but which, as a state,
does not follow the basic concepts of Christianity."[8] The Abbot, as was
to be expected, was attacked for his mental aberration, as one who
had joined ranks with the professional critics of Spain: the communists,
Marxists, atheists, priest-murdering anarchists, near-heretical progressives, Masonic lodges and affiliated groups . . .[9]

While the above currents undoubtedly exist, the Catholic Church
in Spain, as forcefully portrayed by Goytisolo, remains backward
and intransigent, evoking in contemporary form reminiscences of
Pío Baroja, Pérez de Ayala, and Ramón Sender's position on
priests.

Hugh Thomas finds that most Spaniards constantly test reality.
After all, from the sixteenth century onwards, each of the leading
political ideas of Europe has been received with enthusiasm by one
group of Spaniards and opposed ferociously by another, without any
desire to compromise being shown by either side: the universal Roman
Catholicism of the Hapsburgs, the Absolutism of the Bourbons, French
revolutionary liberalism, romantic and then commercial separation,
Socialism, Anarchism, Communism and Fascism: with the exception
of the last-named, these concepts have all been imbued in Spain with
the sharp contrast of light and shade which is the most remarkable

attribute of the Spanish landscape . . . The very sharpness with which these political ideas stand out from each other in Spain is peculiarly Spanish. No one has ever been more absolutist than the Spanish absolutists. The virtues and shortcomings of liberalism are nowhere better demonstrated than by the Spanish liberals. The Spanish Anarchists are the only Anarchists in European history to have made any mark upon events . . . Spain has thus been a litmus paper by which the political ideas of Europe have been tested. And the advocates of each idea have desired to impose their own views exclusively.[10]

In the last few years labor and student strikes, and the concept of freedom of the press, increasingly supported by the liberal priests, have brought new repressions from Franco's police and soldiers. A growing number of intellectuals and newspapermen support the unions in spite of imprisonment and other punishments. Paradoxically, Franco has agreed to a weakening of governmental censorship and a relaxation of his intransigent position in religious, political, and social matters, but even in 1967 these changes were being made grudgingly and slowly. Two factors have promoted changes. Increasing tourism has not only filled Spanish coffers, but has furthered Spain's exposure to new ideas and the acceptance of a neo-capitalistic industrial concept of society. Twenty-five years of enforced political and social conformity, and the departure from Spain of many of its finest intellects, have deadened Spanish capacity to create a truly national or revolutionary resistance. The refugees, themselves divided, have no real power base in Spain from which to operate, and whatever the form of government which replaces the Franco dictatorship, it is doubtful that it will be one of true democracy where the Spanish people can vote without limitations, even though, in some instances, opposition candidates are now allowed to run for office. (On July 22, 1969 Franco proclaimed Don Juan Carlos, 31, his successor). The "Twenty-five Years of Peace" have inculcated a conformity and obedience in the vast majority of the Spanish people, and the traditions of the Inquisition, furthered by Franco, will not easily disappear. It is doubtful that in future novels Goytisolo will substantially change the implacable, photographic reproductions of the period between 1939 and 1963 or do more than reflect the illness of a nation which seems to have lost its soul.

CHAPTER 2

Literary Backgrounds and Structural Experimentation

I The Twentieth-Century Novel

MANY SPANISH critics during the twentieth century, including Torrente Ballester, José María Castellet and Ortega y Gasset, have claimed that the Spanish novel is a dying form, a declaration difficult to accept as one considers the richness and variety of Spanish fiction. The anguished novels of Unamuno seeking the identity of man's soul in the universe and its immortality; the tortured, exotic, esthetic contributions of Valle-Inclán; the action-packed picaresque versions of Baroja; the well ordered, classic, religious works of Ricardo León; the impressionistic though often static portrayals of Gabriel Miró; the psychological, humorous, and ironic works of Pérez de Ayala; the realistic and humorous interpretations of Zunzunegui; the surrealistic offerings of Gómez de la Serna and Benjamín Jarnés, the most ardent novelistic followers of Breton and Eluard; the outpourings of the many women novelists from Concha Espina through Carmen Laforet, Elena Quiroga and Ana María Matute; and the novels of writers of the fifties and sixties such as Miguel Delibes and Rafael Sánchez Ferlosio are throbbing with life and meaning. Of the living novelists, with the exception of Goytisolo, only Ramón Sender, who has lived in the United States for many years, and Camilo José Cela have achieved world renown as novelists.

In 1944 the Nadal Prize, created by the publishers of the Barcelona review *Destino*, in memory of an employee, Eugenio Nadal, helped to stimulate new novelists. Their works dealt, for the most part, with the Civil War and its effects, although many, fearing the censor, chose safer themes. Many of the young writers lacked the necessary background and culture to write novels. Since the Civil War more than two hundred new novelists have appeared to compete for some fifty national prizes for fiction. Nevertheless, since one cannot live in Spain from the sale of novels, most writers earn their living in other professions. Many of the novels, including some of Goytisolo's, are published abroad because Spanish censorship will not accept the work, in spite of stylistic disguises and subtle symbolism used by authors to convey their message. As Janet Winecoff points out, "Many young novelists questioned felt a sense of mission or duty to speak out . . . a drive toward social reform."[1]

However, not all current novels are direct attacks on the status quo. Juan Antonio Zunzunegui continues the realistic novel in the nineteenth century tradition; Ricardo Fernández de la Reguera emphasizes history; Max Aub, an exile in Mexico, and José María Gironella, among others, continue to write novels about the Civil War.

In the early forties Cela's *La familia de Pascual Duarte* (*Pascual Duarte's Family*) set the tone with its *tremendismo*, a narration of the terrible events of our time in a naturalistic and existentialist manner. In the fifties and sixties the *objetivista* novel, an objective account of facts and a sober description of the common traits of everyday life of ordinary people, implied strong criticism of the grey, somber, and hopeless atmosphere in which Spaniards lived, not a sharp departure from the hopeless atmosphere painted earlier by Camilo José Cela. To the ardent objectivist, nevertheless, a human being was simply one more object to be photographed in a depersonalized universe.

Many generational distinctions are possible. José María Castellet calls the writers born in the fifteen years between 1906 and 1922 the "generation of the war"; he labels the next generation, born between 1922 and 1936, which began to write about 1950, the "generation of the half century." The latter, he feels, show a superior culture and a restlessness about their profession which the novelists of the war generations did not have.[2]

The contemporary novel reflects the continuing dichotomy of the concept of "two Spains," the one a Spain of rigid catholicism and *hispanidad,* the Spain of the Cid and of that nineteenth-century defender of tradition, Menéndez y Pelayo; and the other, the Spain of the nineteenth-century Krausists,[3] the Institute of Free Learning,[4] the students of Giner de los Ríos, the seekers of broadening cultural contacts with Europe. Confusing the broad dichotomy were a series of splinter groups fighting one another within both Spains, the Catholics, the Monarchists, the Falangists, the Freemasons, and the Anarchists. Generally speaking, however, one can speak of an official and intolerant Spain, committed to a consistent dogmatic Catholic faith and opposition to individual freedom and dignity; and the Spain of the *pueblo,* of the ideas of the Spanish Republic, a confrontation which reached its climax in the tragic Civil War of 1936-1939.

Of all the contemporary angry young men, Juan Goytisolo is perhaps the most important and the angriest. Born of Spanish, Basque, and French ancestors on January 5, 1931, in Barcelona, he lost his mother, Luisa Gay, in an air raid by Franco's forces, in 1938. His father, a retired chemical factory executive, was imprisoned during the Civil War. Goytisolo lived in a small village in Catalonia, in a farm house owned by his father. It served as a school for refugee children during part of the war, a setting he used in writing one of his novels, *Duelo en el Paraíso (Sorrow at Paradise House).*

Goytisolo studied law in Barcelona, Madrid, and Paris, but he spent more time, by his own admission, in drinking than in studying. He was uninterested and a poor student. "My father sent me to study—I didn't study. I passed the day and the night in bars and I was bored with it all."[5] He was dismissed from various colleges, apparently for "anarchistic" ideas, but his experiences there gave him the material for many situations and characters of his first novels.

Goytisolo became interested in writing at an early age. At eleven he tried to compose a novel about Joan of Arc and the French Revolution, "packed with crime, robbery, violence and incest; it filled with horror all who read it."[6] His was a literary family. His maternal great uncle, Ramón Vives, was a famous Catalan poet. An older brother, José Agustín, born in 1928, is a well known poet, and his younger brother, Luis, born in 1935, has written some excellent fiction. Juan helped found the Tertulia del Turia in Barcelona in January, 1951. The other charter members were Ana María Matute, Lorenzo Gomis, Mario Lacruz, and Juan Germán Schröder. In 1952 Goytisolo won the Joven Literatura (Young Literature) Prize for a short story which the official censor did not allow him to publish.

In 1956 Goytisolo went to Paris. Since 1957 he has lived there permanently, with the exception of trips to his home in northern Catalonia, to other parts of Spain, and to Cuba. He has a position with Gallimard Publishing Company and has been instrumental, with the help of his friend Maurice Coindreau, in arranging French translations of works by Elena Quiroga, Ana María Matute, and Miguel Delibes,[7] and promoting the Spanish novel abroad.

Goytisolo represents much that is typical of the new writers in his interpretation of a Spain haunted by its Civil War memories and subjected to a political and religious censorship. Ramón Sender, according to many perhaps the greatest living Spanish novelist, said that "he is without a doubt the best of the young Spanish writers."[8] José R. Marra-López felt that Goytisolo possessed "the greatest innate gifts in the genre of the whole group."[9] Although Goytisolo's friend José María Castellet thought that Ana María Matute, the best of the women novelists, might give Goytisolo competition and that *El Jarama* of Rafael Sánchez Ferlosio was the "best example of an objectivist novel to date," he admitted that Goytisolo occupies "a prominent place,"[10] and that he has "a poetic preoccupation and a solid and rigorous technical construction."[11]

Goytisolo realizes that his work stems inevitably from the brutality, indifference, helplessness, and cynicism resulting from the Civil War and the death and destruction it caused. He wrote:

Many of those who are now writing novels were only children during the Civil War. With the eyes of children they saw, calmly, atrocious things. They forgot them. But there was a moment in their lives, as they grew up, in which they suddenly remembered them again. And they remembered them more and more as their bones grew harder and their blood richer. Then, not to forget these things—that would have been impossible—but to free themselves, they began writing novels. After the first wave, of short duration . . . which described the crimes . . . the crushed homes . . . the second wave arrived, slower, more powerful, that which relates what has been destroyed and what has been awakened in consciences.[12]

His novels, in their effort to define the contemporary Spaniard, extract incidents from his own experience. Even though he claims that a complete realism is impossible, that absolute truths are difficult to accept and that a real novelist must accept various possibilities, in his novels he traces the development of his generation from youth to maturity as he describes the adolescent misery, part self-aggrandizement and partially self-disparagement, and the weakness and strengths, such as they are, which are part of the fabric of Spanish society. Constantly, in his novels, the theme is one of contrast between the world of reality and the fairy tale world of make-believe, of innocence and fable. His characters seek escape from their tragic world, through travel to Italy, romantic escape to America, living behind a series of masks, creating unreal worlds of the imagination in which to live, and refusal to grow up. The persistent theme accounts for overused symbols and stylistic monotony, from time to time, which several critics have commented upon. As he explains, "When I began to write I was twenty years old, and I wrote what I knew best. This explains the autobiographical character of my first novels. In reality I did not know anything beyond my social milieu before I wrote *La resaca (The Undertow)*."[13] In most of his novels he sought to connect the war and present day Spain, and he wrote *Duelo en el Paraíso (Sorrow at Paradise House)* as "a caricature of the war . . . Then I had a tendency to grow tender over the characters, children and adolescents. Now I know that the problem of infancy is only one particular aspect of the problems that face our people as urgent matters."[14]

Yet Goytisolo admitted that he found in the actions of children "a sort of microcosm of adult life. Spanish children in particular have a knack of exploiting the world of their elders."[15] Other contemporary novelists such as José Luis Martín Vigil, Sebastián Juan Arbó, Ana María Matute, and Miguel Delibes emphasize the ills of youth, a characteristic of most twentieth-century Spanish fiction. Through the eyes of children and adolescents the authors present a varying but pessimistic view of injustice and misery they find in contemporary Spain, a land of unfortunate children, torn apart by adult emotions of love and hate.

Goytisolo's preoccupation with truth caused him to examine the opposing forces engendered by the war, which helped him view clearly the tragedy of humble, unglamorous lives, and the capacity for suffering shared by all human beings. He writes of anguished times, defections from human dignity, nightmare experiences of a disintegrating society, crudities and violence, and a repudiation of traditional values. The unbelievable poverty to be seen outside the large cities, the temporary hovels erected by homeless people, and the tomb-like government housing are as grotesque as the fantasy creations of the characters in some of his novels, and some of the situations he creates.

Critics, for this reason, have questioned the reality of his protagonists. Yet what may seem false characterization may also be explained as the reality of an unusual situation brought about by a Civil War and life under a dictatorship. Also, although he breaks with the customs of the past, as a member of a new generation, he has obviously read Spanish picaresque literature and the works of Pío Baroja and Valle-Inclán. His heroes resemble traditional *pícaros* who also lived in a Spain of hunger and violence, although Goytisolo's protagonists present a greater self-analysis, emptiness, anguish, and lack of hope in the spiritual crisis through which they pass. Castellet claims that Goytisolo's novels belong to the category he calls "historical realism" or realistic social realism.[16] It is true enough that his novels present real geography, real history, real roads and place names, and real current events, but he sees them often as through a deforming mirror.

Goytisolo properly belongs to the generation following the *tremendista* one, after 1950, which Pérez Minik shows writes an exaggerated and tense prose. "This adjective element, which seems a mere technical fact, carries within it important substantive values . . . the inheritance of 'tremendism', plus the powerful influence of the police novel or the Yankee films about 'gangsters'."[17]

II Foreign Influences on Goytisolo's Works

American novelists have left their mark on Goytisolo. He copied John Dos Passos in his slice of life technique, leading in and out of the time stream in a lengthwise time direction. William Goyen's *The House of Breath*, Carson McCullers' *The Heart is a Lonely Hunter*, which was an "astonishing revelation" for Goytisolo, along with *Reflections in a Golden Eye and The Member of the Wedding*, and Truman Capote's *Other Voices Other Rooms* and *The Grass Harp*, influenced Goytisolo. He identified with Capote and McCullers through their tales of troubled youngsters growing up. He claimed that William Styron's *Lie Down in Darkness* would have made Flaubert grow pale with jealousy. The novel which most impressed him, however, and one from which he borrowed some techniques, was *The Sound and the Fury* by William Faulkner.[18]

Goytisolo also uses American words and sentences to flavor his novels and to reflect the growing importance of the United States in current Spanish literary realism. Many of his characters speak a language liberally laced with Americana, names such as Betty, Gerald, Ellen, Vicky, and George; products such as Chesterfield, Lucky Strike, jeep, Coca cola; American performers and institutions such as Grar (*sic*) Gable, Walt Disney, *New York Times*, and Middlebury College in Reading (*sic*); vocabulary such as cowboy, manager, party, penalty, pioneer, barman, whisky, and a series of phrases such as "Wat is the matter with his?" (*sic*); "Hotel confor, verigud misis. Non espansif. Gud"; "Here is very bad. Do you like it?"; and "She is not beautiful, but she is interesting."

The American himself for Goytisolo is an ugly, drunken, destructive, sexually aroused buffoon. His characters view him as the one to blame for everything (the Americans may even have an atom bomb hidden on their ships). American women are easy to take to bed. Rich Americans are easily duped. Americans pay well (rich Americans are liked by some Spaniards). Americans spend most of their time visiting bars. Americans discriminate against Negroes. America is full of gangsters. Americans exterminate Indians. Even when Goytisolo does not present them as downright deceitful and drunk, Americans are unappealing, with "rosy and inexpressive faces" or "doll-like eyes." In short, the moral decay which Goytisolo describes in Spain is intensified because many of the younger generation are changing their ways and imitating the wrong things, especially Americans, who will not help the unhappy heirs of a land destroyed by hate and violence where true communication and understanding are almost impossible. Thus, while rejecting Americans, American social, political, and economic policies, he accepts American literary tradition, seeing it as the synthesis of an older European one with American revolt.

Goytisolo was impressed by the French writers Proust, Malraux, Laclos, Flaubert, and especially Gide. Pavese and Vittorini of Italy complete the major influences on him.

Goytisolo has also been compared to Alain Robbe-Grillet, and at one time he considered himself an objectivist novelist and disciple of Robbe-Grillet. In his early comments on the novel, Goytisolo praised Robbe-Grillet's renovating effects and even accepted the latter's exclusion of the psychological novel, seeing in it a kind of development of Ortega's concept of "dehumanization." He considered (very briefly) that Robbe-Grillet was his magnificent mentor and stated that "in order to achieve his objective—a chemically pure novel—the author must dehumanize himself."[19] Since 1959 Goytisolo has had various disagreements with the so-called objectivist writers. He rejects Robbe-Grillet's excessive objectivity and stresses his lack of lyrical and esthetic intention and unity of form and content. One of his earliest differences with Robbe-Grillet about the "new novel" was his refusal to accept uncommitted description. For Goytisolo the novel had to mean social commitment. Moreover he could not accept impassive objective descriptions of reality. In all of Goytisolo's novels one finds a lyrical, poetic note, whatever the appalling circumstances. Goytisolo includes sentences such as: "On the horizon . . . some quiet little cottony bellflowers like beards of spun sugar," or "The cloud which raced through the sky splattered it with rapid shadows which adapted themselves to the undulating configuration of the earth." His lyric evocations, present even in the reporter-type novels he has written, differ as greatly from Robbe-Grillet's movie camera techniques as they do from the evocation of the countryside and old towns treated by the Generation of '98. His geography is largely that of the contemporary city, its districts, and its social problems, which contrast with evocations of decaying villages of a former Spain.

We may say then that Goytisolo does not really write an objectivist novel or even a social-objectivist novel. Although he makes use of movie camera technique, he cannot efface himself completely in his reproduction of reality, nor can he treat humans as objects. He tries to be objective and invisible and to give what Camus labeled an "objective account," but he is obviously involved. He finds it hard to divorce form from content, style from human beings and their moral miseries, as he describes the physical aspects, gestures, and emotions of his characters. He presents us with a series of shifting views in the belief that more elements will aid the moral perception of good and evil, as well as stylistic emotional and intellectual complexity. Thus, the urination on sidewalks and other apparently meaningless acts and grotesque behavior found in his novels convey a voiceless protest of the dispossessed in a false society supported by shifting ideals, against which the integrity of each individual act must be measured. He portrays them, too, as a demonstration of the spiritual decay and death to which Spain has succumbed.

But Goytisolo's principal objection to Robbe-Grillet's objectivist novels is the latter's contention that literature may not serve a political cause. Goytisolo himself feels that this may be possible in France, which has political freedom lacking in Spain.[20] In Spain social groups cannot represent their feelings or defend their interests freely, and the writer then must change into the spokesman for their sentiments and interests, serving as a kind of escape valve. Goytisolo hopes his literature will mirror the deep struggle of the Spanish people for their freedom, and so he writes politics, in spite of himself, and feels "we shall live for a long time pursued by politics."[21]

Manuel Lamana, who took part in anti-government activities and was himself a refugee in France at the end of the Civil War, explains further differences between the French and the Spanish situations. In the post Civil War period and the Second World War, the French youth had a free choice between moral suicide, as defined by Albert Camus, and a new system of values based on their war experience, occupation, and concentration camps. But the Frenchman had his country and the enemy as a point of departure. The Spaniard, on the contrary, lacked common ideals, since he was facing not a foreign enemy but rather his relatives. Brothers fought each other, and internecine reprisals, jail, hunger, and misery were the order of the day.[22]

Goytisolo finds it essential, then, that his novels serve a social purpose, whereas Robbe-Grillet feels that the social importance of the novel at best is indirect, since the novelist cannot intervene in the history of society but only in the history of the novel. For this reason, and because of Goytisolo's involvement, the explanation that Goytisolo has attained a certain notoriety by his social combativeness, an apparent desire to shock, and "alliance with the objectivists in Spain and France,"[23] refers to a youthful position since rejected by Goytisolo. He uses visual imagery of cinematic origin, but he sees beneath the surface qualities of objects and cannot accept Robbe-Grillet's view that the world is neither absurd nor significant. He rejects the label of social combativeness, seeing his task as that of projecting, with artistic integrity, common experiences of ordinary people and the realities of their everyday life in simple terms.

Goytisolo realizes the risk of revealing a trivial and insignificant reality through the use of objectivist techniques and refuses to play a kind of game by pretending to ignore the very facts he is presenting, that is, imagining a situation and feigning ignorance of its structure. He attempts to achieve a kind of social realism which takes into account the historical moment in which he lives and his membership in the human race. He is concerned with social progress, and reflects his own particular moral conscience in attempting to fulfill the function of justice in which he thinks authors must be involved. His is not a destructive proletarian propaganda, although for some, he is a communist or the equivalent. Goytisolo rejects political labels, preferring an artistic autonomy in his description of human society and its problems.

III *Goytisolo's Polemics on the Novel*

Goytisolo's ideas on the novel as expressed in his *Problemas de la novela* (*Problems of the Novel*), 1959, and in *Insula*, ideas which he has since redefined and changed, brought him into conflict with a number of critics. At that time he believed that the objectivist novel, based on a synthetic and real appreciation of man's conduct, was the only efficient means of writing fiction. The contemporary Spanish novel must portray Spanish man, in much the same manner as the picaresque novelists reflected Spain in the sixteenth and seventeenth centuries. The novel must be humanized and show us society, not as it believes itself to be, but as it really is. The writer may not manufacture a reality; he can only mirror it, for the theme determines the technique. A truly successful contemporary novel must combine this reality with lyrical elements, a synthesis which is quite difficult to achieve. Above all, literary creativity must relate to social motivation.

His arguments recall an earlier debate between Ortega y Gasset and Pío Baroja. The latter felt that art was life, that all technique and emphasis on art were without any importance. For Pío Baroja, novels were based on "observation of life" and were a kind of "reporting" of things, scenes, and descriptions made from direct impressions. He refused to look from art to life but viewed art from life, the center of the human problem.[24] Baroja felt there was no single type of novel, that the genre is multiformed, in constant formation and fermentation, that it includes socialism, psychology, philosophy, and adventure. No single technique suffices to cover all its forms. Even lyric poetry may be incorporated into the daily life of the novel. Baroja admits the possibility of what he calls the "parnassian" novel, of little interest to him, and believes that every novel has its own type of skeletal structure, although some novels may be characterized by their lack of such a framework, being biologically an invertebrate animal rather than a vertebrate one.[25] He said once that he had the hope, perhaps a comic and chimerical one, that "the Spanish reader thirty or forty years later who may have a less mannered sensibility than the one of today and who reads my books, may appreciate me more."[26] In spite of his differences with Ortega, the latter called him the "least understood of the writers of the period."[27] Baroja elaborates on his theories of the novel in a series of works: *La nave de los locos* (*The Ship of the Fools*), 1925; *El tablado de Arlequín* (*The Stage of Harlequin*), 1904;

Las horas solitarias (The Solitary Hours), 1918; *Los amores tardíos* (*Tardy Loves*), 1926; and the fifth volume of *Memorias* (*Memoirs*), 1948. Baroja's novels convey, in their spontaneity, a direct message to the reader. His descriptions are objective without dramatic emotion, and his short, almost monotonous sentences serve an esthetic function, that is, to set off the author's message or idea. Thus Baroja's novels have a structure of sorts, although the novel may represent life itself as it unfolds before its protagonist. Goytisolo accepts Pío Baroja's general premise that literature is life, but he also involves himself in structural and technical experimentation to a degree unknown to the earlier novelist.

Ortega y Gasset in his *Deshumanización del arte* and *Ideas sobre la novela (Dehumanization of Art* and *Ideas On the Novel)* pointed out that the novel was suffering a crisis, that themes were becoming scarce, and that only refinements of techniques were being practiced. He came to be, for a group of writers, the proponent of the novel as something mental, cold, and objective. Goytisolo, rejecting what he terms a picture postcard nationalism or one disguised by folklorism, tremendism, or *costumbrismo*, stresses the importance of the pueblo, painted with all its problems, hopes, and anger. He finds Ortega's *deshumanización* an interference between the author and his public, nor is he impressed by the refined esthetic novels of Benjamín Jarnés or the popular ones of Felipe Trigo. He admires, instead, the novels of Galdós, Pío Baroja, and Cela, as well as the picaresque tradition. Ortega wrote only for the *minorías* (minorities) and felt that art should be directed to them. What of the majority, asks Goytisolo.

The novels of Gómez de la Serna and Benjamín Jarnés differ little from the arty works of Giraudoux and lack national interest. They wrote a kind of universalized, mannered, monotonous novel, in the manner suggested by Ortega. To become truly universal, says Goytisolo, the Spanish novel must become both national and popular again, rejecting both the refined productions of writers like Jarnés and the vulgar ones like Trigo to return to the tradition of Galdós and Pío Baroja. In becoming national and popular, the Spanish novel will then once more reflect meaningful contemporary problems, for it is necessary to "humanize or perish."[28]

For Goytisolo, Ortega y Gasset bears the prime responsibility for any deficiencies in the Spanish novel. He created a situation in which Spanish readers of novels looked to foreign works more than to national ones for the satisfaction of their sentimental and moral needs, since foreign productions responded more to these popular Spanish needs than the stylized efforts of Spanish novelists, influenced by Ortega's concept that art was an aristocratic game and that the mediocre, everyday aspects of life had no great interest for authors. Everyday life, says Goytisolo, does not imply vulgarity, but rather is of vital importance.[29] It is the duty of every author to fight against tyranny and try to reveal the truth, no matter how difficult the task. In order to achieve truth in fiction, a dialogue between author and public is necessary, but an author may objectively record exterior actions of characters without entering directly as narrator.[30]

He feels, however, that an author must go to the people to acquire a knowledge of his social role, the sure road to firm cultural values. The psychological novel is not suitable for the poor in spirit and those for whom delicate soul problems have never existed. They are quite often a luxury the poor cannot afford. Therefore, he rejects interior monologue or the introspective psychological novel, which he later uses extensively, as being primarily for the middle class, and he stresses the theatrical advantage in having persons physically present without having to analyze them. (As we shall see, he again fails to follow his own prescription, for he explores time relationships in a technical sense, and employs other modern stylistic devices.) Pace and rhythm are very important in this presentation. He rejects Ortega's concept that ideas, instead of being an instrument with which to express an object, are objects and ends in themselves of our thought. He finds Unamuno's *nivolas* egocentric, but he accepts Baroja's denunciation of external reality.

One of the first to enter the fray against Goytisolo and his ideas on the novel was Guillermo de Torre who rejected Goytisolo's arguments in *Ínsula*. He called it a "manifesto, although it does not carry such a name." While he agreed that one becomes universal by stressing the national, the new realism, he argued, lies in the accumulation of excessive frequent details and dialogues, literary phonographic translations which tend to disfigure and falsify the very reality they seek, following thus in their distortion the very dictates of Ortega they purport to oppose. Goytisolo, he says, suffers a fatal amnesia and is moved by a desire to discover new lands by going over already used-up material. Goytisolo offers a limited message, for his only points are that the novel must be popular and exemplify national realism. What of technique? Max Aub, says Torre, made the same points against Ortega and made them better. Many other writers before Goytisolo have exemplified the realism of which Goytisolo speaks, but Goytisolo himself does not write realism. He writes, rather, "currents of poetization and mythification of the infantile world."[31]

Torre's reaction to Goytisolo's novels recalls his earlier writing on the subject where he states that the novel is at a crisis in its development, indulging in experimental changes, widening its frontiers, erasing limits to such an extent that "could someone specify where the novel begins and where it ends?" He denies that Pío Baroja's works are novels and finds the new realism in Spanish novels a disfiguring one. Torre's test for the novel was to see if the personages have independent life, if they continue to live once the book is closed.[32]

Goytisolo, of course, feels the novelist must be judged primarily by his ability to interweave technique and life rather than by his ability to create fictional characters. He feels that the novel is not going through a crisis but rather through a period of transition, evolution, and the appearance of new forms, and needs, if anything, elevated cultural levels and greater participation by people.[33]

José Corrales Egea, in an article entitled "Entrando en liza" ("Entering the Jousting Field"), entered the debate along with Paulino Garagorri, "Disputaciones orteguianas" ("Orteguian Controversies"), in *Insula*.[34] Corrales Egea answered Torre to the effect that Goytisolo had no intention of writing a manifesto, but that he rejected popularist and nationalistic literature while accepting "popular"and "national" literature. For Goytisolo the period of 1925-1936 reflected nothing. For Torre it represented a vital and esthetic moment. Goytisolo does not deny there were good writers who wrote psychological novels, but there was no real national novel which reflected Spanish reality as witnessed by Spanish novelists. Torre's claim that Goytisolo, by living in

Paris, gave up his national connections is not valid, for, says Corrales Egea, one can write national novels outside of Spain. Far from being selfish, Goytisolo has done much to spread the new Spanish novel abroad.

IV *The Structure of Goytisolo's Novels*

In spite of Goytisolo's insistence on a national novel, he, more than any contemporary Spanish novelist, has experimented with most of the twentieth-century novelistic techniques. Goytisolo employs an unusual amount of dialogue to increase emotional response in his readers, along with social meanings and the reactions they evoke from various individuals. He deals with life rather than language, but his word patterns, images, and stylistic devices help set off his ideas. His dialogue gives an almost dramatic intensity at times to his reproduction of reality and imbues its traditional nakedness with a new and vital passion. His short outbursts, aside from following American style, project the theme of an indifferent universe in an absurd world where intelligence avails little. In projecting his reality he may employ an almost reportorial style; at times he uses cinematographic technique by presenting deeds instead of describing them and trying to inculcate emotion through a narrative rhythm which makes use of the long view, flashbacks, close-ups, and the like. He rejects narrow formulas and tight structures.

Since life is composed of many threads and does not run in a straight line, Goytisolo structures his novels to reflect this. In his use of time flow he creates a deliberate impression, much in the manner of Faulkner, to maintain the reader immersed in his story. He uses abrupt transitions of time from past to future, but he emphasizes constantly the present in which we live, a reality which is inextricably linked to a historical past and a hypothetical future. He views time as a continuity, not as a straight flow, as though events past and future were contemporary. The treatment of time is his dominant concern. Thus he compresses the action of *Fiestas* into five weeks, that of *La isla* (*The Island*) into eleven days, and that of *Señas de identidad* (*Signs of Identity*) into three days, physical limitations which, nevertheless, allow for far reaching and unlimited mental voyages into the time stream.

He views time as a kind of space where one can live, to render account of the seconds and minutes outside of time, and to view the past, present, and future as a unit.[35] His alternation in the time stream allows him to cover many individuals, and more than one generation. This causes, at times, disjointed appearing incidents but gives us a total picture of Spanish society and achieves the psychological impact of continuous creative evolution in the present, which Henri Bergson defined. Time is "a succession of qualitative changes, which melt and permeate one another, without precise outlines, without any tendency to externalize themselves in relation to one another."[36]

Goytisolo impressionistically handles small groups of people whom he joins and abandons, whose lives intersect briefly, in parallel, contrapuntal plots. Often his characters seem devoid of real humanity and appear to be automatons, but all have relevance to the total structure. Personalities impinge on one another in shifting and kaleidoscopic patterns, but the disparate characters, strands of narrative, and structural complexities are usually untangled, if not completely resolved, at the end of the novel. In early novels he employs a flagrantly bad style, grammatical infelicities, faulty sentence structure, and an apparent lack of careful structural cement. This writing may be a deliberate obfuscation on the author's part, a distortion of the supposed reality he paints. Goytisolo realizes that detailed description may not always give the essence of life; he combines atmosphere, theme, nature, language, popular transcriptions of specialized vocabularies of beggars and others, along with lyrical offsets to the destroyed lives, passion, and blood, much as he combines fantasy with realism.

His is not really a social art in the Marxist sense, for he has combined nature and society in his works to avoid direct propaganda. He is poetic, original, and creative, even though his raw material is not new. His idealistic cause is to dignify humanity in a country whose dominant ideology is dedicated to a suppression of that cause, and it is not surprising that his works are not always pretty, but he finds no essential conflict between ethical and esthetic considerations. His moral commitment to the cause of justice and his hatred of despotism have not led him to employ an exclusively didactic approach, and he has balanced his social message with artistic, lyrical, and poetic concerns.

As we have seen, Goytisolo felt that a change occurred in his writing after 1958 with the publication of *La resaca* (*The Undertow*). Yet Goytisolo cannot escape his involvement in the cultural framework of his children and the Spanish Civil War, and his values stem from that involvement. Stylistically, too, the apparent changes have not been fundamental. In his early works he tried to mold the material of his story to a specific form or style such as cinematographic emphasis or flashbacks, for him a kind of intellectual deformation; that is, by searching for a formal originality he thought he was sacrificing the authenticity of situations and characters. Since *La resaca*, the witness or reportorial novels and personal memoirs about his unfortunately chaotic country nevertheless involve considerable technical experimentation. Goytisolo created innovations within the framework of his cultural values. He started no new artistic fashion, but he achieved a refreshing fusion of the modern and the past, revealing historical and stylistic truth in the picaresque tradition in a new way.

From a chronological point of view, *Duelo en el Paraíso*, 1955, his second novel, should have come first, as it treats of children during the Spanish Civil War. *Juegos de manos* (*Sleight of Hand*), 1954, handles these same children in their adolescence, and *El circo* (*The Circus*), 1957, presents the same generation as young adults. His latest novel, *Señas de identidad* (*Signs of Identity*), 1966, reviews the entire historical, social, and political framework of Spain in the last thirty years and thus analyzes his generation from birth to maturity.

V Some Critical Opinions

Among the critics who have evaluated Goytisolo's novels, many of the Spanish ones, as is understandable, have reacted strongly and often unfavorably. José Marra López accuses Goytisolo of using careless language but at the same time attacks him for having a linguistic obsession for using correct vocabulary, one not usually employed by the people,[37] perhaps a reference to the special vocabulary which Goytisolo emphasizes to reveal his knowledge of the argot of the criminals, the beggars, and the homosexuals in his novels. Eugenio de Nora complains that he uses a great number of archaic words in *Duelo en el Paraíso*,[38] and José María Martínez Cachero faults him for incorrect language.[39]

Ricardo Gullón criticizes Goytisolo for falsification and deformation of his country into a nightmare scene of alcohol and sex.[40] Gullón also feels that Juan Goytisolo is not representative of the twentieth-century novel, in spite of his success in France and America, because he takes events more from literature than he does from life, a literature which is marked by anguish and despair in any event.[41] Goytisolo readily admits that the very selection of portions of reality implies a choice on the part of the author, as he examines the suffering and poverty of people and presents them to the public for judgment, a public which had suffered hunger and death on both sides of the Civil War. He admits also that some of his tormented heroes are reminiscent of those presented in the picaresque offerings of Baroja and Cela, but he says these defeated and disillusioned victims seek for meaning in the only ways they know. Thus he presents them as fragments of a collective mass which has lost its dignity and individuality. In contemporary Spain abnormality remains as a significant factor in the citizens' daily life.

Eugenio de Nora finds Goytisolo to be "irritated, anarchistic, violent, almost temperamental—that is to say, of subjective origin . . . which explains his lyrical escape and disguise . . ."[42] For him Goytisolo is neither realistic nor analytical. Paul West calls Goytisolo a specialist in "the urbane urban sordid" and one who has inclination to "phony melodramatic . . ."[43] He labels his prose gaudy, cinematic, and flamboyant.

Finally, José María Martínez Cachero laments the limiting factors which Goytisolo applies to himself which tend to create a monotonous effect. He decries Goytisolo's long stay in Paris as causing further deterioration in his already faulty Spanish, and feels his literary fame is swollen out of all proportion by matters which are far from literary. He fears that Goytisolo's real possibilities as a narrative writer may be damaged by "a dangerous technical and thematic mannerism."[44] To all his critics Goytisolo replies that literature and life are inextricably intertwined, and he wants to show man, not only as he should be, but as he really is. He rejects the well ordered universe of classical art, style, and experience, although he accepts the ethnocentric implications of Spanish national traditions. While this has not won him applause in Spain, yet in France and in the other countries, along with Camilo José Cela, he has the greatest reputation of any Spanish novelist.[45]

CHAPTER 3

The Early Novels (1954-1957)

I Sleight of Hand (*Juegos de manos*), 1954

IN MADRID, David, a law student, is greatly influenced by Agustín Mendoza, a would-be painter and the leader of the group of youths with whom David associates. He is well liked by most members of his group, but he suffers anguish at not being the best at everything he undertakes. He tries hard for a real identity in a difficult world. He is idealistic and believes in social reform. The poor workers in the factory and in the field love him, but he feels guilty because of his own privileged social position. Placid by nature, he loses his first sweetheart, Juana, to his friend Agustín, and his other girlfriend, Gloria, to Jaime, arrested for the illegal possession of concealed weapons. Yet he continues to see Gloria without resentment at having been used by her to further her plans.

The wild youngsters of the group, all products of a Civil War environment they experienced as children, feel that Spain is being run by "old goats" who exploit youth, the same old goats who fought in the Civil War and caused a million deaths. The gang decides to kill a minor political official, Francisco Guarner. It is a murder planned without revolutionary convictions on the part of anyone except Ana, but rather through a feeling of disillusionment, as a symbol of rebellion against their middle-class backgrounds, and to experience a kind of gangland existence.

In a crooked card game David is chosen to be the gang's instrument. His very goodness arouses the enmity of Luis, a member of the gang and Gloria's brother. The latter, fearful of the fatal card, arranges with Uribe to manage a sleight of hand which will give the fatal card to David. The sensitive David is unable to carry out his task. One or two of the gang members know what Agustín's reaction to David's failure will be, but they are unable to warn him effectively. Agustín kills David and then gives himself up, as other members of the gang disperse.

It is the air of suspense, the dramatic intensity, the feeling of immediate reality, and the violent insight into human beings which give life to the somewhat slight plot vehicle. The characters engage in a ceaseless round of frantic activity alternating with laziness. They seek in group behaviour a final attempt to live up to the true potential they feel in themselves, to justify their existence, to be something. They search, without knowing what they seek, uncertain, anxious, and disoriented. The dichotomy between what they want and reality as it exists causes an explosion of violence. Unable to identify their vague ideals, they take refuge in anti-social activity against the very world of their elders in which they had learned about cruelty, cheating, lying, and murder, in a Spain without a system of values by which to live, where Spaniards exist in a moral and spiritual vacuum. They vaguely feel they are achieving a kind of identity by throwing stones at beggars and urinating on flowers; they also reject the hypocrisy and false education of their society, along with their families and parents. In addition to belonging through a kind of romantic loyalty to the group or gang, they seek to commit an astonishing act, thus denying themselves the possibility of pardon and cutting their family ties forever.

Goytisolo's adolescents thus lack positive goals which can satisfy their anxieties, and their activities do not really help them. They are sick members of a sick society, and their emotionalized attitudes and social values reflect their maladjustment. They seek socially forbidden goals, not from a sense of ideological commitment but out of frustrations at the barriers imposed upon them. Yet they find difficulty in verbalizing these barriers precisely, for they perceive them only vaguely, even subconsciously, as they try to compensate for their frustration. They are largely paralyzed by guilt feelings, by inadequacies, real or imagined, and by past failures. Goytisolo reinforces their psychological orientation toward the past by his constant time shifts and use of flashbacks.

Goytisolo describes beautifully the process of growing up, of adolescent hate, love, and rebellion, of what he terms the "terrible generation of our time," a generation which seems to have neither the wish nor the will to do anything about their alienation from their world and their society; when they finally act, it is as though unknown forces impel them and limit the practical implementation of their desires and possibilities for self realization and individuality, almost impossible to preserve in a dehumanized, perverted, and grotesque Spain where human values have been brutalized and desecrated. In this world, where true communication is impossible, Agustín achieves brief understanding when he exclaims, "Oh, David, David, I have killed you and without knowing it I have killed myself."[1]

David, in dying, offers no resistance to Agustín, for he feels he may thus atone for his own, his parents', and his companions' shortcomings in a meaningless world. David, allowing for some fictional exaggerations in the descriptions of his overindulgence by his parents and their weakness, may be an autobiographical recreation of Goytisolo and a description of his Spanish world as he remembered it. David recalls a photograph of his grandparents who made a fortune in Cuban property later liquidated by an aunt and uncle. The same incident is recalled in later novels, *Duelo en el Paraíso* and *Señas de identidad;* and in *Pueblo en marcha* (*People on the March*), a narration of his trip to Cuba in 1962, he reveals this to be a true part of his own family background.

Having been robbed of their birthright in one way or another by their parents' emotional shortcomings and hypocrisy, these adolescents feel they have never had a childhood, that they live in a world where nothing ties them to the past, nor even to the future. Agustín's parents, overly loving, had become puppets in his hands. He hated and mistrusted his father for his weakness, and his mother for the ambition which led to his dissociation of personality. David, sickly and weak, continued so because his parents overprotected him and led him to view his home as a refuge from the brutal world. Raúl laments his father's ideas on happiness, which define it as tranquility, rest, and lack of pre-occupation for the future.

The adults such as don Sidonio and doña Cecilia, Luis's parents, ask a price that youth cannot pay, and unable to adapt to the bourgeois values and lack of true ideals, unable to affirm or articulate what they stand for, victims of anger and a sense of helplessness, each member of the gang uselessly seeks a meaning in his world. Luis Páez, cowardly, dirty, envious, selfish, and lazy, a product of parents unable to control him and from whom he stole, becomes an aimless wanderer. Ana, the only one who finally matures, becomes a dedicated revolutionist.

The most impressive character, in a sense, Eduardo Uribe, David's cousin, is a drunken, effeminate, perhaps homosexual weakling who briefly tries to be a man and warn him but who succumbs to his own weakness and fear, seeking escape from the world and from himself in a make-believe existence of disparate masks. He is a strange character, sensitive to music, to the touch of fur, to the sight of colors, and to the secrets of nature. He bedaubs prostitutes and his own body. He suffers as he cheats to give the fatal card to David, an action he takes through fear of Luis Páez. He cures Rivera and sits by his side for days; yet he vomits easily before ideas which repel him. He drinks constantly, dances, sings, speaks to himself and feels a compulsion to reveal his life, real and invented, to everyone. His room is a strange combination of objects, mostly false, as the face he turns to life is false. His phony pistol, instead of bullets, shoots rag flowers, photographs of Naples and Vesuvius, and pairs of lovers. His room also contains talismans, stones, astrological tables, and magic objects. He symbolizes a negation of reality; he must disguise things, for he cannot face certainty nor reality. "Reflected in an unframed mirror—there were dozens of them throughout the room—he saw himself and knew he was drunk. He became aware of the public. He was acting."[2]

José María Castellet rejects *Juegos de manos* as a "compendium of the men of our land and our days," and finds it unrealistic as a portrayal of Spain.[3] Yet José Luis Cano points out that Goytisolo obviously intends to portray life in Franco Spain, since David represents himself as the editor of *El Alcázar*. Cano feels, however, that as a drama of universal youth and rebellion it could also exist in any other country.[4] Those who are not Spaniards find it difficult to accept the novel as reflecting a generation, in spite of the Falangist reign of terror. They cannot conceive of such a lack of human values, the ugliness and filth which Goytisolo claims is current Spain, where violence and hate fill the air. Goytisolo presents it as a true picture of the generation he labels "second wave . . . the one that tells what is destroyed and awakened in our conscience."[5] Goytisolo shows us the world as he believes it to be, the nature and limitations of human beings, although in the process, in spite of the artistry and truth, he does not remove himself sufficiently from his characters to obtain the appearance of objectivity. Castellet finds that Goytisolo enters the thoughts and feelings of his characters through the use of certain metaphors and by uncovering their thoughts and emotions.[6] Yet José Luis Cano says that it has "artistic truth,, sufficient so that the story interests and even impassions us."[7] Whether one finds it an exaggeration or a magnificent picture of the terrible youth of our time, Goytisolo himself says that "I am not concerned with Spanish politics. I am a writer transposing into literature what I have seen and experienced. *The Young Assassins* is not autobiographical, but is concerned with a *milieu*—the sons of the well-to-do bourgeoisie —which I knew very well when I was a law student in Madrid eight years ago."[8]

Juegos de manos, written in 1952 but not published until 1954, took third prize in the Nadal contest, although it was far superior to either of the novels which placed ahead of it. It has been translated into many foreign tongues and published in English in 1959 as *The Young Assassins.* Even in that year the implications of the novel (the first of a long list in contemporary Spain to deal with adolescent rebellion and criticism of the status quo) were hard for the Spanish jury to take. Indeed, the Spanish version was changed because of the pressure of censorship, and the French version by Maurice Coindreau is more brutal and direct, in keeping with Goytisolo's intentions. The language is clear and to the point, although Castellet finds it "vacillating, ineffective, and not very spontaneous."[9] Generally Goytisolo follows the mid-century generation of exposition which seeks to shock through stylistic as well as thematic changes. The hopelessness of the situation is conveyed by descriptions of environment and characters such as those where paint drips a gummy secretion on the sidewalk "like mascara smeared by tears." "The fog yellowed about the bulbs of the lamps." "Dressed in an extravagant manner, he wore his coat unbuttoned and his pants covered with dust. His shirt was also opened and his tie hung badly knotted. His face had a grayish withered color, as if his bloodless skin were absorbing the indecisive shade of the last shreds of the fog." "The moon bathed with its indifferent patina the equestrian statue and the asphalt center of the plaza. Like a shadow he slipped between the sleepy houses until he was lost in the gray reflection of the row of arches."[10]

Maurice Coindreau, among others, has commented on the relationship of Gide's *Les faux-monnayeurs* (*The Counterfeiters*) to Goytisolo's work,[11] and the dual culpability of the counterfeiters of both generations, as fathers and children counterfeit justice, ideas, and convictions, Parents, blind to their own crimes, are shocked by their children's defects. Both writers seek to redefine the novel as a reflection of reality as seen through the eyes of contemporary man. Thus we have a clash between the real world and the individual's representation of that world. Goytisolo evolves his personalities much as Gide evolves those of his two adolescents, Olivier and Bernard. While there is no exact parallel in Goytisolo with the developing novel of Edouard, Gide's mouthpiece, in both each character holds a special pattern in the novel's time sequence. Goytisolo plays with time and space as he shifts and refocuses from past to present, from generation to generation, from character to character.

He analyzes both internal and external reality, using a direct narrative based on the memory of his characters, but at the same time, as he confronts the reader with their direct experiences, he describes as author narrator. In most instances, however, the characters present their feelings so forcefully that they displace Goytisolo to the periphery of the narration. Ana's case is representative. She reveals for Francisco Guarner an aversion which stems from an association with the founding of a group of cheap houses near her own, an infantile memory recalled from her eighth year. "Ana—it was curious how she remembered it after so many years, apparently engraved it in her memory with images of fire—was dressed in a little blue coat with a round collar . . . Tears ran down her cheeks. She understood nothing. She was only eight years old. The delegate—Ana told him—was called Francisco Guarner, and with the passing of time he symbolized for me the compendium of what I hated most. He is kind, tender, and affable with children. He has it all: the superficiality, the education, the money and the manners."[12]

Agustín asks her if her rebellion began at eight, and she replies that it was much later. For seven years she lived a choking existence under the absolute influence of her mother.

My mother was absurd, . . . Her teaching had something infinitely consoling, like those honorable manuals which teach one how to overcome timidity, or the art of succeeding in business. They were grotesque, empty of significance, like empty husks . . . My mother was more ambitious and intelligent than my father, who was, in the final analysis, a simple carpenter and he respected as something established her natural superiority. He had turned over the task of educating me to her completely and never trespassed on the limits he had voluntarily imposed on himself. Mother was pleased by his understanding and when she spoke of him she called him 'your poor father.'[13]

So the years passed. Ana recalled (again specific times are important to Goytisolo) that eight years before, when she was fifteen, she attended the catechism of a group of rich girls on Sunday mornings. Among them was the slender, elegant Celeste who invited her idly to visit her some day. She did, met the rich and empty companions who patronized her, and "I felt that there blossomed in my soul the flame of hate: I wanted to die and the earth to swallow me."[14] Some days later a friend of her father, discharged because of some strike in which he had taken part, told her father that in the future world charity should be abolished, a phrase which to the fifteen year old appeared wonderful, even if she did not fully understand it. The next day (as we have seen, Goytisolo moves at will in the time stream) she wanted to know from her father what a revolutionary was. The next night she continued the conversation. Her father told her he had been a revolutionary when he was young (a typical Goytisolo temporal association). Two weeks later she took a job in a factory, a gesture which represented to her a repudiation of her childhood. During that time she began to feel the need for killing, for only through bloodshed could she achieve the right to be a revolutionary. Only she, of all the gang, feels that an ideology that fails to transform postulates into immediate action is harmful.

As can be seen, Goytisolo impresses the time sequences on our minds: "Some weeks before," "after so many years," "I was eight years old," "It was much later," "eight years ago," "the next morning," "the next evening," "two weeks later." Past and present become fused in memory. Goytisolo traps the present moment but adds to the consciousness of his characters the experiences of an unforgettable past which for them, and for him, is an immediate present. He gives us a series of close-ups and fade-outs, flashbacks and zooming camera effects to reveal the responsibility and interrelationship of two lost, and in a sense terrible, generations. Luis Páez deceives his parents, and don Sidonio plaintively cries out: "In my time it seemed to us to be something terrible to deceive our parents. When I think of your poor grandfather . . ."[15] Goytisolo shifts from character to character in the present and then takes us back to examine the origins of each one's revolt. The present for Goytisolo seems to be an abstraction which is as much a part of history as is the past. He shows us the present or a series of "actualities" which succeed one another, but historically the period being examined is immediately past. The reader is made to feel the present as a kind of victim to the past, in a sense devoured by it, especially by the most important event in Spanish history, a war still more "real" than the "present" being lived.

Uribe the actor is almost completely without ties. He acts so much that his fantasy becomes almost a reality to him. He tries to invent a history which will match the real ones of his friends. "When I stole for the first time—he said—I was sixteen years old and in love with a beautiful dame."[16] As David and Agustín recall their first meeting when David was nineteen years old, Agustín says: "I had finished my secondary schooling, remember. When I think of what we were then and what we are now, I am astonished at myself. Hasn't something similar occured in your case?" David replies: "Yes, we have lived very rapidly; without ever looking backward . . . It seems to me that

we have died; that now we are different people." Agustín in
turn replies: "It's only that nothing ties us to the past. Not even
the future. We live for the day."[17]

In *Juegos de manos,* as well as in his other novels, Goytisolo
uses interior monologue, which Robert Humphrey defines as
the "technique used in fiction for presenting the psychic content
and processes of character, partly or entirely unuttered, just as
those processes exist at various levels of conscious control before
they are formulated for deliberate speech."[18] Goytisolo uses both
fully conscious and subconscious monologue to enable us to
understand a character better. At times the guiding hand of the
narrator is apparent, as he introduces the monologue with a
direct transition to interior monologue. Goytisolo, nevertheless,
uses quotation marks to show the first-person narration which
gives us the pivotal point of the crisis to be resolved. Often his
character will employ direct memory and give the reader a kind
of unvoiced soliloquy to reveal the turmoil caused by his own
self-revelation. Through indirect third-person interior monologue,
Goytisolo enters the direct monologue in the first person which
is combined with it. At times he combines historical narration,
indirect interior monologue and direct interior monologue. In
the following passage, David's associations are aided by his self-
induced somnolent condition which makes the penetration of his
mind an easier task.

He tried to remember what had happened and could not. He wanted
to find an explanation, the key to the events of the day, and he looked
around him in search of help. The fragmentary vision of Guarner's
face, his silk beard, his fingers tensed on the gun trigger, formed
separate images which he could not unite. "I have failed," he thought,
"I intended to fire, but I could not." His ideas came to his mind aloud;
he could not avoid it. He repeated them again in a mechanical way
and passed his hand over his forehead soaked in sweat.

"I clutched the revolver with all my strength and, yet, I could not.
When I was a boy I used to say to myself: 'If I have not kissed Juana
before I come to the third house, I am an idiot', and in spite of that
I did not kiss her and I would give myself a delay of three more
houses and still I would not dare kiss her, in spite of the fact that I
was dying to and I had to insult myself again. With Guarner the same
thing happened. I wanted to kiss Juana and I didn't have the nerve.
By this time she must have married a man who knows how to domi-

nate her. She understood things well. If she had continued with me, it would have been a failure. People like me are not for marriage. Gloria also realized that. She says that Betancourt knows what he wants and that I am a victim of life. She scorns me. Maybe she is right and I am not much of a man. In dad's factory the same thing happened. Dad used to bawl the devil out of the employees and I almost died of shame. I wanted to do something that, in their eyes, would separate me from him. I have always wanted to have myself pardoned for *I don't know what.* It is strange, this business of wanting something that one doesn't know."

He realized that he was wandering and fell back on the bed. How heavy his head was. How tired. An idea had just occurred to him, and he muttered it aloud: "I am thinking all these foolish things because I am still dreaming them." To sleep, sleep, sleep, to close his eyes. He opened them again and began to make out in the shadow the figures of light on his bed. During entire hours, as now, he had remained in his room without doing anything . . .

"It is curious that this had to happen, precisely this morning. It could have happened any other day and it wouldn't have mattered. At times it seems that one's body anticipates what one wants. In college I was a model student . . . I do not have initiative like Agustín. . ."[19]

The action, then, as can be seen, is fragmented by time, by character, and by interior monologue, but this fragmentation, criss-crossing, and interrelationship are necessary in order to create the final unity, to build for the culminating temporal moment, the assassination of David, an action which reveals fully the counterfeit aspirations of the would-be revolutionaries and anarchists who live in an absurd world full of such actions. Goytisolo, skillfully using the theory that psychology deals with manifolds of coexisting facts, employs concepts of time and space to enable the reader to understand the spiritual vacuum in which his characters live.

In spite of the bleakness, *Juegos de manos* is not without its humorous notes, although even these have grotesque aspects. Lucía, David's aunt, got pleasure out of watching some priests who lived in a nearby convent, and with whom she successively fell in love. Their toilet facilities were situated under Lucía's observation post, and she became aware of the digestive habits of the priests and the difficulties of some of her favorites. One day David saw her pacing back and forth in great excitement and watching with more avid interest than usual. She had sent the monastery a box of chocolates, filled with laxative, whose effect she had proved by direct observation.

Juegos de manos had an important critical impact. Pérez Minik called it the "best 'black' novel of this cycle. Strange, hallucinating . . . with a confused rhythm but terribly expressive. A good document of this time. It possesses a great social content, is daring and very free . . . At times it recalls a French film of recent times, but we must recognize that there is in it a very Spanish style and origin: a taste for chiaroscuro, of reality tinged with impassibility and scandal, and a good gait along uncertain roads."[20]

John Dos Passos wrote of the English translation that it was the best novel "to come out of Spain in many a year. It seizes hold of the reader with the nightmare force of *Crime and Punishment* or *The Possessed* . . . It has the impact of immediate reality. A vigorous and stimulating and frightening piece of work."[21] Gilbert Millstein was struck especially by "the orderly, artistic contempt with which a very young writer disposed of a generation and a society that had so plainly failed him . . . It takes great skill and insight and maturity not to descend to whining and Goytisolo displays all of these . . . The writing, exquisite in its spareness, its exactness . . . The novel is first-rate; it is, as far as I am concerned, memorable; it may be, for others as well as myself, lasting."[22] Paul Pickerel found it to be: "The best of the recent novels about young people that I have seen . . . It would be an impressive book by a writer of any age . . . There are scenes with almost Dostoevskian intensity . . . Not a pretty or entertaining book, but it has a psychological and dramatic force not often encountered in Fiction."[23]

David Dempsey claimed that it was "a harsh book and a gripping one . . . Once he is warmed up, Goytisolo writes a stunning, successful book . . . A very moving and brilliant book, *The Young Assassins* begins where the novels of a writer like Jack Kerouac leave off."[24] In Paris, *L'Expresse* wrote of Goytisolo that in *Juegos de manos* he possessed "an exceptional discipline which is in itself the mark of a great artistic temperament . . . this first novel goes like an arrow . . . to the truth."[25]

II Sorrow at Paradise House (Duelo en el Paraíso), 1955

In a small village near Gerona in northern Catalonia, Martín Elósegui during the last weeks of the Spanish Civil War has deserted from the retreating Republican Army. As he lies in hiding in a cave, awaiting the arrival of Franco's troops, he hears a shot. He investigates, and stumbles upon a young boy, el Arcángel, who throws a grenade at him. Elósegui finally discovers the corpse of a twelve-year-old boy, Abel Sorzano, known to him. Abel's parents had been killed during the war, and he had been living as a refugee in the home of a half-mad aunt, Estanislaa Lizarzaburu. The house was known as El Paraíso, Paradise House. Martín discovers that the perpetrators of Abel's murder are other refugee children from a nearby school, one of whose teachers, Dora, he had loved, had made pregnant, and then had lost to death in a bombardment by Franco's planes. The Basque refugee children, copying the actions of the adults, kill Abel. Elósegui surrenders to the Franco troops and meets Begoña, a former girl friend and now a Red Cross nurse, and he puts all memory of Dora from his mind. The children are captured by the soldier patrols.

Goytisolo now returns us to an earlier time period in his narrative. Abel, the grandson of Estanislaa's older sister, doña María, learns the sad story of his aunt's life. She had had two sons. David died. Romano, the other son, fell in love with Claude, a young lady whom the mother jealously drove away, indirectly causing her son's death in an automobile crash. With his death she lost her reason. When Abel's parents died, for a time he lived with a grandmother and an aunt and uncle, but when his grandmother died, his uncles were unable to support him. When he came to live at Paraíso, Martín, almost the first person he met, gave him directions as to how to find the house, the beginning of a new life for Abel. As the novel begins, it has, in reality, ended, and Martín has just discovered the body of his friend a few minutes after Abel had been killed.

Duelo en el Paraíso placed third in the *Planeta* prize competition and won the *Índice de artes y letras* (Index of Arts and

Letters) prize from a jury composed of Torcuato Luca de Tena, José María Castellet, Eusebio García Luengo, Álvaro Fernández Suárez, and Antonio Vilanova. The novel was translated into English in 1958 as *Children of Chaos*.

Some striking parallels exist between Goytisolo's novel and William Golding's *Lord of the Flies*, published just one year earlier. The Spanish author's work is perhaps not as profound or original as that of Golding, nor does Goytisolo's novel lend itself so easily to the symbolic interpretations found in *Lord of the Flies*, although both view children as vehicles for creation of myths. Nevertheless, because it treats of reality rather than invention, Goytisolo's novel may be essentially more tragic.[26]

Both deal with the destruction of youthful innocence in a world of evil. Both leave one with the impression of implied hope. In both stories the children lack civilized support for positive action: in Golding's work because the adults are supposedly dead; in Goytisolo's because the adults themselves, the Church and the State, preach the return to savagery. In both, a refuge from the evils of society is destroyed, in one case physically, in the other emotionally. El Paraíso has a symbolic value as a refuge from the war, a place that might have been a kind of Eden were it not for the bestiality of men, much as the Island of the *Lord of the Flies* might have been Paradise. The boys of Golding's novel burn their island. In *Duelo en el Paraíso* they destroy the last chance for happiness in a real world for those at El Paraíso, and attempt to burn the school master and the school, which El Arquero, the gang leader, had dreamed of ruling as a city of children.

The characters are similar. Goytisolo's Emilio and Golding's Ralph repent of what they have done and, in the process, reveal themselves to be human boys. Emilio and Ralph had taken part in a killing and share the responsibility. Both weep at the end for their loss of innocence and at the realization of the evil around them. Emilio may be reshaped. Ralph has learned about life. Ralph also resembles Goytisolo's Abel. He too became a pariah because he was different. He too was hunted and almost killed at the end. Piggy and Abel also have much in common. Both were good boys; both had lost their father and mother; both lived with an aunt. El Arquero and Jack are the same. The former takes over the school as his province; the latter, part of the Island. Both represent the savagery which stems from forces easily released when normal civilization disappears. Both are arrogant and unscrupulous. El Arquero trains the boys as soldiers to take over power. Jack trains his as hunters. Both have rivals: El Arquero, Pablo; and Jack, Ralph. El Arcángel resembles Simon somewhat. The latter is killed when he brings the message that the frightening beast discovered on the island, a beast which has assumed mythic implications in their minds, is really a dead airman killed in the war. El Arcángel is only disciplined when he fails to destroy their enemy, Elósegui. Abel and Simon both have visions. Abel dreams of death, of his unborn brother, and of Romano and David. The rose in his hand, perhaps symbolizing the need for love in a wicked world, has a counterpart in the pig's head in *Lord of the Flies*. In both works the forest is full of voices.

Other similarities may be noted. In both novels the boys regress. In *Duelo en el Paraíso* they wear feathers, in savage Indian style, don masks, and paint their faces. They also wear war paint in Golding's novel. Both deal with the mass evacuation of school children during a war, in one case a postulated Third World War, in the other, the real Spanish Civil War. In one case they are stranded on a desert island; in the other, in a small village near Gerona.

However, some basic differences exist. Goytisolo is not a philosopher. Unlike Golding, he does not stress the need for man to define himself in a changed universe of unknown conditions or concern himself with man's vision of metaphysical evil. Rather he deals with the horrors of what an event which changes a nation can do to human beings in a physical sense. Furthermore, in *Lord of the Flies* the boys have a choice. They may choose Piggy's rational discussion, Ralph's order, or Jack's tribal superstition and human sacrifice. In Goytisolo's novel no real choice exists, for the negative weight of the so-called civilized world is with the children, exhorting them to savagery rather than to civilization. In the final analysis Golding seeks out archetypal patterns of human society and ponders defects of human nature; Goytisolo stresses the defects of contemporary human society.

José Luis Cano has found some connection between *Juegos de manos* and *Les Enfants Terribles* (*The Holy Terrors*) of Jean Cocteau.[27] These works, in reality, have little in common. A more obvious comparison might be made, however, between *Duelo en el Paraíso* and *Les Enfants Terribles*. In both novels school children torture others, and steal; they also exhibit a similar kind of childhood friendship and attachment. The relationship between Dargelos and Paul resembles that between Abel and Pablo. In both novels the gangs are untamed savages. Perhaps the real relationship lies in the penetration by both Goytisolo and Cocteau into the subconscious regions and tenebrous instincts of their children: ". . . they take on the aspect of beings of a different order of creation—conjuring themselves at will an instantaneous coat of bristles or assuming the bland passivity of some form of plant life. Their rites are obscure, inexorably secret, calling, we know, for infinite cunning, for ordeal by fear and torture; requiring victims, summary executions, human sacrifices . . ."[28]

Goytisolo acknowledged the influence on his work of that of Carson McCullers. In most of Goytisolo's novels, but especially in *Duelo en el Paraíso*, one can see the same kind of relationships among people found in *The Heart is a Lonely Hunter*. Each of the Spanish author's characters seeks understanding, love, and meaning in life, and Abel serves as the focal point, much as the mute, John Singer, does in the American novel. Singer dies a victim of his own unfulfilled love, although he has given a certain outline and meaning to the other characters. Among these are Jake Blount, frustrated communist of the big fists and broad shoulders; Mick Kelly, the young girl with hidden longings who matures to face the real world; Biff Brannon, the owner of the New York Cafe who is never quite sure whether he will succumb to bitter irony or faith; and Doctor Copeland, the frustrated Negro doctor who seeks freedom for his people. In a similar fashion, el Gallego realizes his own personality in his relationship to Abel, and Abel needs Pablo, just as Mr. Singer needed Spiros Antonapoulos.

Goytisolo experiments with brief sentences, emphasizes popular speech, gives value to gestures and situations and uses spatial and temporal elements to maximum advantage in his search for time control, as temporal inversion triumphs over chronological life. He employs interior monologue, flashbacks, objective and cinematographic narration techniques. He presents his minor characters, as well as his major ones, in a series of episodes, as each character lives in a special time stream and has his view of the reality being examined. Only gradually do we realize the time sequence and organization. Goytisolo does not immediately clarify the theme, and tries to maintain interest and suspense in his revelation of the background and causes of Abel's death; thus he talks of Estanislaa's past, her two children, ancestors in Cuba and Central America, the recollections of Elósegui, Abel's life in Barcelona, and a succession of impressions held by other characters in his association of past and present.

The old beggar, el Gallego, a veteran of the War of 1898 (veterans and beggars are recurring types in Goytisolo's novels), learns of the death of his friend, Abel. When he is told, el Gallego's mind shifts into a kind of confused dream state at the news of such great emotional content, and Goytisolo effects a deliberate discontinuity. Although the reader has not been in constant contact with el Gallego and has, indeed, just met him, he becomes aware that the character has been living an entire life. The reader adds a dimension in his realization that el Gallego also has a philosophy of life. "(In his head, the themes of love and of death danced grotesquely intertwined: the girl and the soldier, who sought to complete themselves through the union of their two bodies became confused with the face of the recently assassinated boy. The butterflies, the men who marched united, were nothing more than a confused impulse toward death. Everything tended toward it, like the alcoholic toward alcohol, the moth toward the flame, and that which was the object of love one day, was changed into its prey at the end of an instant.)"[29]

The corporal asks el Gallego if he knew Abel, and the old man nods his head without saying a word. Goytisolo then shifts to the beginning of the friendship of the old man with Abel, in a third-person narrative. However, the story is now told from the point of view of el Gallego who himself becomes a third-person narrator, recalling Abel's nightmares and his experiences. In other words, temporarily, el Gallego becomes the author-narrator who is entering the mind of Abel. The two then have a variety of conversations and experiences, which el Gallego recalls, but the past events are presented as though the principal narrator, Goytisolo, as the omniscient author, were simply giving us actions going on at the present moment. Similar shifts of the center of interest and discontinuity occur throughout. One character will ask a question which then gives another the key, as it were, to a host of memories of his association with Abel, usually with such intensity that he seems to be giving a transcript of the passing scene.

As in most of Goytisolo's novels, temporal considerations are dominant. The time sense of his characters slows the rapid pace of the narrative, and the multiple points of view lead to a somewhat incoherent pattern already referred to. His characters do not lead a chronologically complete and coherent life from childhood through the years, but Goytisolo's short-lived time fragments manage to give us the impression of chronological development and completeness, along with a feeling of the historical past and the historical present. This confusion of time is constantly noted by the characters themselves. " 'The execution will be at ten o'clock.' His arrival had disrupted something and, because of it, they had fired at his back.

"In a little bit—he thought—I will have lost my liberty. I will have become a prisoner. He remembered Dora: 'The day the war ends'. As always, making plans for the future, projecting it at a distance. He knew only how to think in the present: he couldn't even succeed in imagining the arrival of the national troops."[30]

Estanislaa, a temporal being as are most of his characters, is filled by time and her contentment; she finds her happiness in the memories which she relives and revives as a kind of continuing dip into the living time stream. Her last words, as the novels ends, are "Once, many years ago . . ."

The work is filled with this recreation of time, not only in constant insistence on phrases such as "two weeks ago," "the next day," "the sun and the clock showed four o'clock," "two years ago," "a week later," "my watch stopped at 2:20," and the like, but recreations such as: "She remembered it as though it were yesterday . . . She recalled the scene clearly . . ."[31] Goytisolo stops the action to invert time and project memories. He uses simultaneous nearness and distance, nearness in time and distance in space or the reverse in temporal spatial terms. He uses a fade-out, dissolving views, and a fade-in to weave the memories of the past with the current action, and his cinematographic technique consists of showing us situations as if they had been photographed by a camera in all their details. The reader supplies imagination and logical deductions as to the causes which produce the effects the author is revealing, but the abrupt transitions in time, where past and present coexist without intervening time passage blocks or transitions, make for a kaleidoscopic panorama, often difficult to follow. "Never had I seen a dawn like that one. Without knowing why I had the impression of finding myself in a strange place. Although the light that entered through the window illuminated the objects weakly, I supplied with cuts from my memory the details whose relief was not yet profiled; the chrome which hung from the opposite wall; a blue advertising calendar. It seemed to me that all was perforce immobile, as if it were awaiting the arrival of a photographer."[32]

As we have seen, as the novel begins all the action has already occurred. Abel is dead and the troops have withdrawn. The war has ended, but for the children a new life of freedom is just beginning. The past, present, and future are inextricably linked, a temporal fusion which fits well into the loose-form construction, as Goytisolo sweeps backward and forward through time and space, implying some hope for the future because of the innocent unawareness of the children as to what their actions really mean, a hope for the future which, as we have seen in *Juegos de manos,* when the children grow up, is never realized. The entire work really forms a long explanation of the opening scene, and it is only at the end that we return to the "now" of the time stream with all loose ends tied together. It is almost a detective story. A crime has been committed, and the reader and the author venture through the minds of bystanders and suspects to discover the motivation behind the act. Since the work is not told in chronological order but in time jumps, the reader sees the character of Abel develop before his eyes.

The flashbacks projected to the future from the past reveal

three generations, that of doña Estanislaa, living in her former grandeur, a past which no longer exists except in her imagination; that of the soldiers such as Elósegui; and that of Abel and the other children. Undoubtedly Goytisolo used his own personal experiences (when he spent time in a country house, owned by his father, near Barcelona which housed refugee children) in writing the novel. The references to Abel's great-grandfather who had disembarked in Cuba and by dint of hard work had left his children two sugar mills and a number of slaves, and other incidents, belong as we have seen, to Goytisolo's own family history. Emilio, the son of Sergeant Santos, and one of the gang, narrates events from his child's point of view and may also reflect Goytisolo's own experiences, and be an autobiographical projection of the author, for it is Emilio who, at the end of the novel, gives a summary of the events: the plans to kill Quantana and Abel, the gathering of arms, the lack of resistance on the part of Abel, and the discovery by Elósegui. We learn finally that it was the Arcángel who threw the grenade at Elósegui. Thus, Goytisolo contrasts time elements, examines the effect of lives and persons as each character relates to another and his experiences within his own world, adult or child, and in the process joins the two worlds. Both are subjected to the war. Both react to it, suffer from it, and hope to achieve freedom from it. Thus, for Castellet, *Duelo en el Paraíso* is "the authentic infantile vision of the war of 1936 . . . the generational testimony of those who were children still at its end."[33] As we saw in *Juegos de manos,* that generation, nevertheless, still felt uneasy and guilty, even though they were not directly responsible for the holocaust.

Duelo en el Paraíso exhibits the same brutal realism mixed with poetry found in his other works, as real characteristics fuse with imaginary ones, and tenderness with cruelty. The children live in an unreal fantasy world of magic and misery, cruelty and poetry, a combination which Nora finds "subjectivized to excess."[34] Yet this grotesque absurdity is exactly the atmosphere Goytisolo wishes to convey. As Quintana, the old professor at the school, exclaims, "It is absurd . . . everything is absurd."[35] In such a world death, peace, poetry, violence, brutality, and anguish may be mixed. When David, Estanislaa's son, died, "the little body lay in the center of the patio, covered with flowers. Floating in a sea of petals, only his face and hands showed through."[36] If death brings peace, life brings anguish in the tortured society which was (and is) Spain. Abel, the innocent, as a victim reveals the guilt we all must feel in a disintegrating phase of society reflected clearly in the abnormal behavior of the characters.

Usually nature descriptions are employed by the author to contrast the natural peaceful world with the artificial destructive one of man, although it may be threatening by its own nature. Goytisolo often combines his descriptions of nature with that of the War, in this novel, or to show man's miserable social state in a supposedly civilized country, in other novels. Thus we find that nature, reality, poetry, and humanity reinforce one another to create what many have seen as a "poetic realism."

The sea was a sheet of leadish color in which the waves seemed petrified. In the sky the clouds gathered menacingly, and, as if launched forth from all that waiting, an airplane . . . flew over their heads . . . "The war, the war," exclaimed the children. The appearance of the shooting star had provoked an effect of catastrophe; gusts of wind uncombed the pines of the path and the sea covered itself with furrows of foaming spittle. The airplane pirouetted over the bay and the heart of the children beat with fear when they saw it discharge its bombs: one, two, three, four. Almost at the same time, little clouds in the form of puffs rose from the breakwater until it fused in the grey ashy color of the west.[37]

In addition to direct comparison and fusion with the Civil War description, Goytisolo makes oblique references to that unforgettable catastrophe. "A quiet magic atmosphere seemed to suspend, miraculously, all the valley above the desolation and the war. The sun bathed the garden in which the automobiles were parked, the ivy which covered the façade, and the basin of the fountain. Against the horizon some quiet and cottony bellflowers raised their heads like beards of spun sugar."[38] "The sun was about to reach its zenith and huddled the shadows at the feet of the trees. The dew drops which spotted the forest humus had disappeared with the dampness. A white butterfly flew to his pauldron and lazily shook its wings."[39] On occasion the author returns to nature to find or set a mood which has no immediate direct or indirect relation to the social, political, or economic environment. "Behind the undulating slope of the fields, the sea was a dense obscure mass. Night had fallen while they worked and the entire countryside was sunk in a bed of shadows."[40]

Spanish tragedy involves a constant relationship with death; it is death which is almost the unseen protagonist of the novel. Refugees are machine-gunned by airplanes; people are summarily executed; "every five minutes a trainload of corpses pulls out." When Estanislaa's husband dies of cancer of the throat (Goytisolo was impressed by terrible physical ailments such as cancer which recur constantly to victimize certain characters), with her last money she hired automobiles to bring the friends of her husband to his death bed. The rows of empty automobiles arrived, for her husband had been forgotten by the world. Estanislaa had lost both of her sons, and her husband, Enrique, had betrayed her in many ways, all contributing causes to her half death, as a mad participant in a living world. Filomena, her servant, had lost five children. Dora, the school teacher whose life had been unhappy, dies in a bombardment, the child she was carrying still unborn, much as Abel's mother had died with his unborn sibling inside, for even the unborn are victims of the war.

Abel himself perishes to become one of the death statistics the children constantly heard broadcast over the radio along with news of murder, destruction, spies, and terror. If, as the radio said, adults should fight and take justice into their own hands, children should show initiative too, in order to secure their freedom. By killing Abel, whom they accuse of treason, they achieve a kind of purification and enact a grotesque parody of the war of their elders. The radio insisted they should form their own police, learn to denounce all traitors, and to punish companions who turned out badly. Having no war of their own, they invented their own punishment, their own traitor. Pablo had formed a criminal band before being evacuated. The school children formed a similar band, turning to el Arquero for leadership. Abel Sorzano, the boy from Barcelona, came from a landowning family which had had money while they suffered hunger, and so he had to die. Ironically Abel had written letters to generals, dreaming of contributing his share to the war effort. Living in an age of violence and war, the children soon discovered that he who was not an executioner ran the risk of being a sacrificial victim. Life for them was not a precious commodity, for they lived in a country where "symbols lost their value and the only thing remaining was man reduced to his skin and bones."[41]

The children, then, have to assume the functions of adults, for life passes rapidly, and war situations induce rapid mental if not physical growth. Pablo Márquez, Abel's friend, is typical. In December, when the Nationalist bombing began, he returned home one day to find a pile of ruins. His father, mother, and entire family had died. He fled in panic, wandered through various districts, and was finally caught by a policeman when he stole some food. At first he stole from necessity; later he stole through perversity.

The novel ostensibly relates the life and times of Abel and those around him, but in reality it may be viewed as a kind of fable on the death of the Spanish spirit. Each character individually provides us with one sequence of a bitter experience leading to either a physical or spiritual death. Elósegui represents the composite life of the average soldier during the Spanish Civil War. He may or may not be the fortunate one, in that he survives to experience a kind of life at the end. Abel does not fit into a world in which he is trapped, as was David in *Juegos de manos*, not so much by the young anti-social monsters under Arquero's leadership as by the circumstances of his time. He played a game of make-believe in a real world of life and death where the distinction between reality and fantasy was also a thin one. So el Arquero dreams of a city formed by children, much as Mendoza in *Juegos de manos* dreamed of a society of anarchy. Both represent anti-institutional attitudes, very much like those found in Baroja's novels. Weird characters, the favorite crude material of Goytisolo, also parade through his novel, pathological types who represent the wrong kind of adulthood in a Spain of solitude, cruelty, and hunger. Goytisolo has fused political and social truth with a moral and esthetic one, and has transformed a reality of experience into an ideal reality of a work of art

III *The Circus* (*El circo*), 1957

In the small coastal village of Las Caldas, the people are celebrating the feast of the town's patron saint, San Saturnino, the central event of the year and in their lives. Utah, a bohemian painter who is returning to his village from a trip, finds himself impoverished by his extravagance. He hopes to borrow money from the rich man of the town, don Julio Alvarez. Given to daydream fantasies in which he plays a variety of roles, he keeps sending to his wife mock telegrams about the arrival of a "dangerous assassin."

A young tough, Atila, exerts great influence over a friend, Pablo Martín, whom he prevails upon to help in a robbery of don Julio while the latter is at the fiesta. Julio returns unexpectedly from the traditional dance to honor the saint, interrupts the robbery, and is killed. Utah, still the play actor leading a make-believe existence, finally arrives at Julio's house after a series of adventures. He discovers the body and, confused himself as to what is reality, claims to be the murderer and is accused of a crime he did not commit.

El circo, which Goytisolo called a "farce which finishes badly,"[42] ironically dissects Spanish society, the young idlers and drifters, juvenile and adult delinquents. The novel follows the same technique of interacting lives we have seen in his earlier novels, and the title itself comes from the grotesque aspect of much of the action, which might more easily take place in a circus atmosphere. Utah especially is a kind of clown. A bohemian spendthrift who spends his life hidden from reality behind a series of masks, he cannot himself distinguish between the real and the unreal. He is so self-hypnotic in his mania that he is able to escape temporarily into a dream world and fuse it with reality. His confusion affects others and thus he had bewildered a Basque major with his fantastic tales. "Dazzled by the argument, the major offered him for some days the rich hospitality of his villa, until frightened by the number and voracity of the creditors who deluged him, he took him in a jeep to the airport; once there, it was not difficult to find a pilot friend who transported Utah to Barcelona, hidden in the cabin of the airplane."[43]

Utah, a kind of anarchist, is happy in his dream world, and he scorns the ordinary people of society.

> Separated from them by a curtain of glass, dressed in a recently made overcoat, his muffler and his gloves, he felt disposed to judge them crudely, with a mixture of high disdain and delicate horror. Ordinary. That is what they were: ordinary people; working all day with their dirty hands and their faces covered with grease; collecting bonuses for each child; joining some union. Since his father said that they were socially useful, he felt very proud of being a parasite: a hydra with a hundred feet with the face of a white water lily, superbly useless, treacherously false.[44]

As he rejects his bourgeois milieu, society, in turn, cannot pardon him or find a place for him. Ultimately, then, it must share part of the responsibility for his rejection and failure. Utah never forgets that he is an actor. As he goes to Julio's house he looks for some revealing signal from the stage director who will acclaim him a magnificent actor as the people come out from behind their curtains and blinds to applaud his fine acting. José Luis Cano says that, "Although the author has not wanted to lend Utah a symbolic value, for me it is evident that he symbolizes . . . the rebellion of fantasy against the growing flatness and mediocrity of existence."[45]

Like Uribe in *Juegos de manos*, Utah reveals a lack of responsibility for other victims of society. He offers no aid to his wife, Elisa, in her struggles against creditors. She earns a small salary as an underpaid dress designer, but they must sell their household furnishings to survive. Utah's only solution to the menace of life is a further escape into a new fantasy. Something stronger than he obliges him to don a succession of masks. Although some of Goytisolo's characters are only two-dimensional, Utah, as Goytisolo describes him and through his own thoughts and the reactions of his relatives and those he encounters, is a multi-dimensional character almost larger than life. In refusing to face his adult responsibilities, in continuing to be a child, he suffers the consequences of what to society must seem grotesque actions.

Yet Utah brings happiness, too, for he allows those around him their moment of escape from a humdrum existence. Elisa is happy with him. For her he represents more than a loved one; Celia, his friend, also admires him greatly. The latter's sister, Matilde, cannot understand this admiration and exclaims, in her bourgeois righteousness, "I do not know what interest a man without a job or money can have for you and who, moreover, is half nuts."[46] The extravagances of Elisa's husband increase her love. She accepts the risk of living with him, renouncing the advantages of a normal existence, preoccupied only by her husband's happiness and that of her daughter, Luz Divina, who also adores her father and cannot understand the town's adverse reaction to him.

Utah is not the only play actor. In a series of vignettes Goytisolo shows us the needs and rejections of each character. Flora needs escapes of various kinds and tries to hide behind youthful clothes and alcohol, but she finds small consolation in either a secret life or religion. Don Julio fools himself with his false concept of charity, as he pontificates about the evil "reds" during the war, and how difficult it was for solid citizens of society. Juana, illicitly in love with Atila, wants to escape her humdrum existence. She and her sister Vicky hate one another and their parents. Vicky finds recognition in threatening to reveal her sister's behaviour. Atila, of a poor family, had suffered hunger and thirst. He wanted the good things of life without working for them. His plans are not fully achieved. Luz Divina also needs recognition and suffers her disastrous party, which nobody attends, while Celia seeks a vicarious love through her romantic illusions. The saddest failure, perhaps, is that of the doctor, Don Elio, known as el Canario. He had been kind to the poor, and his liberal ideology had led Don Julio and some of the other good citizens of Las Caldas to believe he was an anarchist. His son died in the war, and he found no joy in his daughters who did not understand him. The world for which he had fought and suffered had been destroyed. "And there remained only the other world, the present one, a grotesque caricature of his dreams, like an empty and pretentious husk, empty of all significance."[47]

In this empty world, however, all seek compensations of one kind or another. Some seek friendship; some seek love; others see material wealth as an answer to their emptiness, their feeling of being hemmed in by or estranged from society. Thus Pablo needs Atila who pokes fun at him and treats him badly, much as Abel in *Duelo en el Paraíso* needed Pablo and felt he was the center of his universe. This need for security and love in a world of hate and fear recurs constantly in *El circo*. Yet in one way or another, the characters all prefer ignorance to truth and are incapable of guiding themselves or of leading new Spanish generations.

Another security, aside from friendship and love, lies in the Church, as symbolized by the feast of San Saturnino, the village patron saint. From the solemn Mass at ten by a representative of the Bishop to the great dance at eleven at night, the Church offers the people a feeling of belonging—at a price, of course. This explains the ferocity of the audience when el Canario, who had been drinking, opposed himself to the universal acclaim afforded the representative of the Church; it is the Church that serves as one uniting thread through the three parts of the novel.

The deformed and disintegrating society portrayed by Goytisolo resembles the "esperpentic" inventions of Valle-Inclán. Max Estrella, the protagonist of *Luces de Bohemia* (*Lights of Bohemia*), a play by Valle-Inclán, gives the definition of the *esperpento* as the concave side-show mirrors where the boundaries of the possible and the credible are blurred;[48] the author achieves a real distortion enhanced by a further fictional distortion. If the *esperpento* was conceived as a grotesque stylization, it also was based on social involvement and concern, the twisting of real historical events, a technique evolved from Quevedo and Goya among others. Only a deformed esthetic can give us a true picture of Spain, for Spain itself is a grotesque deformation of European civilization, say Valle-Inclán and his followers. Goytisolo, by showing the reader a conflict between the twisted "real" reality and his imaginative reality, manages to create a composite picture of the Spanish circumstances of his time. Goytisolo views the Spanish tragedy as though through a deforming mirror. He sees the lack of values in modern life and attacks the institutions such as the Government and the Church, which contribute to the chaotic situation. Whatever the reality and whatever the mirror image, both realities fuse and become almost interchangeable because of their fundamentally similar twisted identity.

Perhaps because the entire novel is an examination of what Goytisolo obviously considers a schizoid country living in a dream world, fewer lyrical descriptive passages are necessary to set off the stark reality. Nevertheless, even in *El circo* several such passages occur. "In front of the automobile lights, the highway seemed a long white ribbon. The banana trees which bordered it, left leafless by autumn, with bare stumps defended themselves fearfully from the light, elevating their branches with terrified gestures. The plain stretched out, dotted by dozens of little lights, toward the black curves of the mountains, and the moon was reflected among the clouds like a splotch of light, round, silvery and brilliant."[49]

Goytisolo does not always use clear narrative bridges in *El circo* and often dissipates even his tenuous narrative connections. Nevertheless, in spite of the discontinuity of structure, we learn all of the plot elements in a variety of ways. The author talks to the reader in the third person, but we also enter the minds of the characters, listen to their dialogue and their information. From them, as well as from the author, we hear about events at the same time that we view the passing scene, at whose periphery Goytisolo vaguely maintains himself to allow the characters to project their points of view. From time to time he will use a dissolving fade-out. Thus Elisa, overhearing her daughter defend Utah against the charge that nobody wanted to lend him money and that he had gone to Madrid to ask for alms, thinks—Goytisolo leaves his third-person narrative, and she thinks in third person—that he may find friends to help him. Immediately we change to a third-person account by Goytisolo of what Utah was doing that afternoon and of his encounters. Utah becomes the central actor and engages in dialogue with a variety of people.

From the scene in which we see Utah attempt to hire a car to come to Las Caldas, we shift to that village and to don Julio's interview with Pablo Martín, the son of Elpidio, the owner of El Refugio bar. The one connecting link is the village to which Goytisolo makes a sudden space shift, rather than a slow fade-

out. In his discussion with Pablo, Julio explains his viewpoint
of the Republic and the Civil War. The scene shifts to El Refugio where Elpidio insists that Utah will pay his debts or go to
prison. Celia enters the bar, and we learn through the ensuing
conversation of Pablo's relationship to Atila and his group. We
also learn of the grandfather's association with el Canario, the
drunken, broken-down doctor. The scene again shifts to a cock
fight where Atila and Pablo discuss the planned robbery; we
then turn to a discussion of Luz Divina's party; we shift once
more to Utah and his trip; we meet Flora, who is relating to a
servant her association with Beremundo, a young man who entered the village with the Nationalist troops at the end of the
War and remained to work. In the next room Flora's sister,
Regina, recalls the same events in a different light. According
to Flora, Beremundo had to leave when his mother was dying.
Regina knows it was an invention of Beremundo to escape involvement with Flora. We learn of Flora's feelings of frustrations and her fantasies about her attraction to men. The scene
shifts to Juana, Atila's girl friend, and then to Celia, the school
teacher, and her sister Matilde. Celia goes to Utah's house, where
in a conversation with his wife we learn that don Julio has been
making advances to Celia. Throughout the rest of the novel Goytisolo utilizes the same technique. We learn all the details but
not in a chronological development.

The reader has the impression that Goytisolo was experimenting
with ways to prolong the suspense through the plot compli-
cation because the central structure was a weak vehicle. Nevertheless one receives what might be termed a reproduction of
reality and a fairly good concept of what Goytisolo was trying
to convey, in this "farce which ends badly."

Goytisolo uses both fully conscious and subconscious monologues to enable us, not so much to simulate the stream of
thought, as to give us an insight into the character discussed.
These monologues may take place at any time, but are obviously
more easily triggered by moments of psychological distress.
Goytisolo uses direct, first-person interior monologue, indirect
third-person interior monologue in many combinations with psychological impact. At times he intervenes as the omniscient author;
at others he does not.

The following passage illustrates one aspect of the author's use of interior monologue. Worried over Utah, Elisa thinks about the problems involving her husband which her friends have been relating to her. We achieve direct entry into her mind. The monologue, in this case rather than a loose chain of associations, concerns one theme, basically: her happiness with and love for Utah and her desire to protect him. Entry into her mind is shown by italics, when the thoughts are especially important. At times Goytisolo uses quotation marks; for the most part he avoids truncated sentences and the ellipses often associated with the technique of interior monologue.

Life, magnanimous and forgetful for many, could suddenly change into something terrifying. For some time now, when friends came to tell her of the madness and follies of her husband, Elisa had limited herself to replying: *Don't worry about me. I know perfectly well what I am doing.* It was all the same to her if Utah washed his feet with champagne or jumped rope with the kids in the park. Living with him was like walking a tightrope. Elisa gladly accepted the risk. *I don't care if he is like that. I love him.* And with a disdainful smile, she had renounced the advantages of a normal existence, preoccupied only for the happiness of Utah and her daughter: *In spite of everything, every day I feel happier, more closely linked to them.* She knew that, surreptitiously, her family was talking of having him locked up. Using her happiness as a pretext, they tried to prevent his future bankruptcy. Besides, for some time now, his health had gotten worse: the cirrhosis the doctor had warned about months before was becoming apparent with all its symptoms. Elisa knew all this and didn't care. *Utah is as defenseless as a child, but I shall fight for him until the end.* Nobody, nobody would take him away from her. "Before I let that happen I'll hang myself from a tree," she said.[50]

El circo, part of a trilogy based on the message and implications of Antonio Machado's "Mañana Efímero" ("Ephemeral Tomorrow"), is perhaps Goytisolo's weakest novel. Yet it exhibits one positive aspect of hope which the first two novels lacked, for as Machado said:

> "The vain yesterday will give birth to a tomorrow
> empty and 'happily,' passing."

IV   *Fiestas, 1958*

Fiestas contains four interwoven stories which concern the lives of the Gorilla, Pipo, Pira, and Professor Rafael Ortega. Ortega, a Republican sympathizer and humanitarian, lived in Pipo's house and taught at the Institute. He lost his position because he refused to march with his students in support of a religious festival. He managed to survive by giving private lessons. An old friend had sent him his son to be looked after, an opportunity Ortega welcomed. However, the son encountered Benjamín, the town homosexual, and blamed the professor.

Pira, a pretty ten year old, dreamed of joining her father who had disappeared ten years before. She pictured him as living in an Italian castle. Selling her wordly possessions to obtain money for the trip, after being frustrated in her dream of winning a big lottery prize, she met a perverted French beggar who offered to take her to Rome. He attacked and murdered her.

Eduardo, known to his friends as Pipo, is a twelve-year-old boy who associates with a giant of a man known as the Gorilla. He wanders the wharves with his friend and meets drunken beggars, gypsies, and prostitutes. He steals from his grandmother and spends the money with his friend. One day, another friend of Pipo, González the policeman, makes Pipo drunk and leads him inadvertently to betray the Gorilla who had previously committed murder.

The Gorilla had had a series of love affairs, including a more or less permanent liaison with Juana who had given him a son. Formerly he had had a wife for whom he had gone logging in Africa. There he had a loyal native mistress, but he abandoned her to return to his wife. During his absence, she had taken up with his brother. Discovering her betrayal, he began drinking and whoring. While with a woman on the beach, he killed a policeman who interrupted them. For a time he enrolled in the Foreign Legion, but later he returned to Spain. He worked as a fisherman, met Pipo, and led his strange and rather free existence until Pipo, who knew his secret, betrayed him to González.

Other plot elements involve a Religious Congress held in the town, and the existence of a hated colony of poor squatters, Murcians who have traveled to Barcelona to look for work. As the Religious Congress reaches its peak, the squatters are dispossessed from their shacks, as the Church and Government remain indifferent to their plight, and the rich and respectable, in a gay holiday mood, help celebrate the Congress.

Fiestas was written before *El circo*, in 1955, but it was not published until 1958. It was banned in Spain and finally published in a faulty edition in Buenos Aires. Goytisolo later rewrote the entire novel for Dell Publishing Company in what he felt was an authentic version. Thus we have the strange situation of a novel, written in Spanish, being published in its first authentic version in the United States. Another edition has since appeared in Spain. Using the faulty edition for their criticism, many have commented on the inaccurate language and the grammatical and stylistic infelicities. Eugenio de Nora, who made the same comment about *El circo*, finds a further fault in *Fiestas* in that Goytisolo has made little change in types and situations from previous novels.[51] Warren Eyster states that it is a very poor novel and "a waste of time" and reminiscent of the worst sociological novels written by Upton Sinclair. He feels furthermore that "his [Goytisolo's] mind seems more juvenile than his years."[52] Offsetting these rather negative views, Ramón Sender (perhaps Spain's greatest novelist of the twentieth century) says of *Fiestas* that it is a "model of harmony, sharpness, love of things and beings, originality of vision . . . *Fiestas* is a brilliant projection of the contrast between Spanish official and real life."[53]

Fiestas opens the trilogy in homage to Machado's famous poem, "The Ephemeral Tomorrow," and Goytisolo completes it with *El circo* and *La resaca* (*The Undertow*). In this novel Goytisolo examines an important conflict between two antithetical realities, that of a Religious Congress which brings an outpouring of joy from the citizens, and that of the Murcians who live, suffer, and die in a poor section of Barcelona. Goytisolo attempts to show the existential impossibility for communication between these entities and among themselves. He wrote to his friend, Maurice Coindreau, that "I have tried to combine the realism of the action with a poetry which draws its roots from

[68]

the action itself. The subject of the novel is the isolation of people lost in the delirious atmosphere of the Congress. I have sought a technique which would express my idea: everything ought to finish by being blocked, the solitude, the impossibility of breaking the barriers . . . fear being the common denominator of all these solitary lives, beaten, damaged by the fireworks of a holiday which is not theirs."[54]

Goytisolo employs subtle touches to convey his opinions. He shows a sign, put up by the Franco government, which has become weatherbeaten and been replaced by a sign with a pretty blonde advertising Coca Cola. The implication which may well be read into the substitution is that the United States is supporting and maintaining the Spanish government. In the same way, after revealing a group of ladies running after the Bishop, curving their delicate necks in order to kiss his ring, he immediately shows us don Paco in the act of feeding a group of hens who come running up to him to be fed, curving their necks to reach the feed.

Not only do the poor Murcianos lose to the Church, but all the characters lose something to the Church and to their society. Ortega loses his position, if not his idealism; Pipo, his physical and spiritual innocence; Pira loses her life; the Gorilla, his freedom. The spatial focal point for the action is the apartment house on Mediodía Street where all the characters relate to one another through Pipo, Ortega, and the binoculars of Arturo, the embittered cripple. The entire action takes place in the five weeks which lead to the culmination of the Congress, the event which dominates the entire novel. The restricted spatial and temporal environment leads to a scenic intensification, although some characters seek to operate outside the spatial restrictions. Even when they do, however, like Benjamín and the Gorilla they are limited, the former by his aquarium, the latter by his docks and bars. Temporally, however, they are free to explore, and both Benjamín and the Gorilla, through their memories, move through time at will.

Goytisolo shows us the futility of human lives and the troubled existence of Spain where man has become a being incapable of true revolt. He manages to mix successfully the experiences of children and those of adults in his strange amalgam of fantasy and reality. The Gorilla, a giant in strength and size, is himself a strange combination of brutality and tenderness, and resembles Utah of *El circo* and Uribe of *Juegos de manos* as an actor at times unable to separate reality from make-believe. Like Utah he is not quite believable. A man of irreflexive violence, he finds difficulty in expressing himself and living his freedom.

The author reveals the same poetic interludes and fusions found in his other novels, as beauty and ugliness, poetry and reality are combined throughout. "The sea was immobile like a black mirror: the lights were reflecting on the water like streamers, forming and dissipating in frequent shreds."⁵⁵ "When he woke up, the sun was already coming up among the shrubs and the air was clear and clean . . . Nearby he discovered a couple asleep in the act of kissing; further on, a drunkard remained clutching his bottle. The turf was sown with papers, lunchboxes, pieces of glass, ashes. After the maddened confusion of the night before, the silence seemed marvelous to him. Full of the night's dew, the leaves seemed swollen; the grass was spotted with butterflies; hidden in the foliage an infinity of birds chirped."⁵⁶

Goytisolo says that *Fiestas* deals with "moral, physical and social loneliness."⁵⁷ The vulgarities, constants in his dialogue, show the author's desire to reflect realistically the behavior of classes with which he is dealing. Among his characters are: Piluca, who seeks escape from dull routine by living vicariously on her cousin Pira's fantasies; the sadistic doña Francisca and her henpecked husband Enrique; doña Cecilia, dying of a tumor in her throat and living in a dream world; her frustrated and useless husband Francisco; their son Arturo, an almost malevolent cripple who lashes out at the world to ease his own pain; don Melchor de la Cueva, the mayor's delegate who wins the big lottery; Benjamín, a homosexual caught in a web of loneliness; Juana, one of the poor Murcian girls; Norte, the Gorilla's friend whose wife had abandoned him; Antonia, the servant woman in Pipo's house who develops cancer of the brain; and Pipo's senile grandmother.

Don Paco's eyes fill with tears when his tomato plants are damaged, but he is uncaring about the poor Murcians and their expulsion from the shacks. Pipo's grandmother knows that he takes her money, but she is too weak to stand up to him. Doña Cecilia can only cry and wait for death. She, like the other adults, is unable to give the children the discipline, warmth and love they need, and she represses the desire to communicate and confide in others. Benjamín, the homosexual, stresses the necessity for manhood, and unable to be manly himself, encourages Pipo to be strong and ignore those who would take him to hidden places.

Pipo, a child without security, looks for it in the magic association he has with the Gorilla. Yet with approaching adulthood comes submission to society and conformity to it and to the Church of his fathers. He realizes that it is absurd to try to live in fantasy, and faces the future as it is. When at the end of the novel Ortega reproaches him about his Church participation and the implied betrayal, Pipo informs him that it is a holiday. Ortega looks at him sadly above his glasses, his face even older than Pipo remembered it, his suit more worn looking among all the people dressed in their Sunday best, and observes bitterly: "The fiestas of some are not the fiestas of all." Pipo feels guilty about his daily thefts and his neglect of Antonia. He cannot understand how he had been able to act in such an unworthy manner and how he had allowed his obsession and blindness to carry him to such an extreme.

Bitter tears of repentance and correction blurred his vision of Mediodía street beneath a screen of tawny rays. The happenings of the evening, like all his previous life, seemed to him suddenly, something very remote. The spectacle of his sleeping district filled him with tenderness. He imagined his grandmother praying for his return and Antonia sobbing and scolding him; the professor stubbornly determined to change the face of the world, and Arthur aiming at the hill with his glasses; the deaf-mute little gypsy waving his little plate, and Benjamín, shut up in the interior of his aquarium. It was *his* district, the place where he had been born, and would die, perhaps, of old age.[58]

All the characters live in what to them is an absurd world from which they seek a way out. Pipo looks for escape through the Gorilla, and Pira weaves dreams about her imaginary father. They fail in their attempts to live life as they would have it, victims of society and of the system. While the Murcians suffer and die, the legate at the very moment of their expulsion climbs his throne of gold and purple and gives his benediction to the people. Everybody suffers an explosion of fervor which he cannot contain, as the tears flow. Under the Church and the Government, says the author pessimistically, life has come to a dead end. He thus finds he has become entangled in the fabric of his own style which involves a conceptual parallelism of physical misery and death and spiritual suicide and loss of identity.

The shifting focus makes the novel difficult to follow at times. Many of the characters serve on the periphery of the main framework as channels of information to the reader and the first introduction of a major figure. Many are only two dimensional; some are sketched to show a salient feature or characteristic, but lack a complete life of their own.

Goytisolo starts *Fiestas* with the announcement of the big lottery. As the children gather around the truck, he produces Pira, who in turn is focused in Arturo's glasses. From Arturo it is easy to transfer attention to the lives of some of the other characters, but Pira remains the central figure in Chapter I. In the second chapter Goytisolo presents Pipo, his home life with his grandmother and the servant, and through Pipo, in a third-person narration by Goytisolo interspersed with dialogue between Pipo and Benjamín, we learn of the latter's contact with Pipo the year before. The point of contact with the present which causes the brief journey to the past is Benjamín's request to Pipo to deliver a message for him. Pipo then meets the Gorilla at his boat and goes off with him to a cafe. Pipo is the central figure of the chapter. We meet the professor in Chapter III, learn of his hopes and dreams, and meet his friend's son. Pira and Pipo have a brief contact. We learn of the Gorilla's experiences with doña Rosa, owner of the cafe; with Juanita, and Pipo's role in their relationship. Chapter IV presents a great number of the minor characters and their problems as well as Pipo, the Gorilla, and Juanita. Chapter V concentrates on the Gorilla, his present adventures and his past life. The next chapter presents all of the principal characters as well as many of the minor ones, achieving a climax with the death of Pira. In Chapter VII Pipo betrays the Gorilla and matures through that betrayal and ensuing realization. The final chapter concerns the procession and Pipo's encounter with the professor. Throughout the novel, however, the two major counterpoint themes are the displaced Murcians and the religious festivities which serve as a backdrop against which the characters reveal their frustrations, cruelties, and idealism.

The somewhat sudden ending reveals Goytisolo's difficulty in terminating the novel through a slow resolution. Pira dies; the Gorilla is jailed; Ortega loses his post; Pipo gives up his youthful innocence. Nevertheless, the author shows his serious concern over their possibility of choice and action, as he examines the relationship of his characters to the painful world they inhabit.

V *The Early Novels—Summary*

Martínez Cachero divides Goytisolo's work into three periods: the first that of *Juegos de manos* and *Duelo en el Paraíso;* the second, the *Mañana Efímero* trilogy; and the last, his later works.[59] Goytisolo himself feels that in his early novels he tried to mold the content to a determined form or style involving interior monologue and the like, creating a kind of intellectual deformation "which is perceived in all my novels before *La resaca;* seeking for a formal originality I sacrificed authenticity of situations and characters. Now (with the publication of *La resaca* [in 1958]), I believe that the theme necessarily determines the technique."[60]

Many groupings of his work are possible, including the one followed in the present book of placing all his novels before *La resaca* in one division. No essential differences are observable between the author's first two novels and his next two, and in spite of Goytisolo's feelings in the matter, there is basically less disparity between his early works and his later so-called documentary novels than is commonly supposed. The themes of the early novels, including an autobiographical milieu which the author apparently feels he abandoned with *La resaca,* are repeated in later works.

In his early novels the poetic description of nature to set off the somewhat brutal human environment; the insistence on details, perhaps without the level of photographic intensity or objective documentation of *La resaca;* the confusion of fictional and nonfictional elements; the temporal excursions; and his own occasional identification with his characters contributed to Goytisolo's thematic structure. The early Goytisolo cannot hide his idealism nor his anti-totalitarian viewpoints; nor can he, given his background, forget the horrors of the major event in twentieth-century Spain, its personal consequences for him, for his friends, for his country, and the inevitable implicit guilt which he and all Spaniards must share for the continuing indifference to the dignity of mankind. Goytisolo offers no viable solutions, indeed, no solutions of any kind, but he obviously wants a more just social order which will not produce young assassins, a caste society, or wars where children and adolescents are the principal victims. As José Francisco Cirre has shown, Goytisolo starts off in many of his novels with a real situation peopled by real characters, but at times he changes from reality as it is to reality as it ought to be.[61] Although he identifies somewhat with David, Abel, and Pipo, he seems to feel no real tenderness for his characters; or if he does, it seems less important than his insistence that his characters function as victims of their environment or man's wickedness.

In dealing with his defeated and disillusioned victims of society, Goytisolo soundly assesses the need for security in an uncertain world. His youngsters seek out those who symbolize strengths which they themselves lack but admire. Thus, a favorite situation in Goytisolo's novels concerns the influence exercised by a dominant personality over another: Agustín on David in *Juegos de manos,* Pablo on Abel in *Duelo en el Paraíso,* and Atila on Pablo in *El circo.* The author was to repeat this formula in *La resaca,* in the relationship between Metralla and Antonio. This security is one which their parents were unable to give them. Often these parents are viewed, not as evil, but as ineffectual bunglers, for example, Agustín's father in *Juegos de manos* and Francisco in *Fiestas.* Goytisolo was to repeat this stereotype in later works also. Still another standard situation found in these novels is the search for satisfaction of psychological desires in an escape into fantasy, which may temporarily, if not completely, satisfy the needs the characters cannot assuage in a real world. Uribe in *Juegos de manos,* Utah in *El circo,* and, to a certain extent, the Gorilla in *Fiestas* view life as a stage on which to perform.

Goytisolo employs a style in these novels reminiscent of some classical Cervantine techniques such as the tertiary or quaternary devices and accumulation of words to further an idea's emotional impact. Whatever the reasons, dozens of combinations appear in each work: "a path made of arms, legs, thighs and human faces."[62] "Pancho appeared through the door of the cafeteria dressed in a cowboy suit: wide rodeo hat, checked shirt, leather jacket, and Texas pants."[63] "What power does it have inside, what does it do inside, what does it think inside, what does it machinate inside?"[64] ". . . covering her with kisses in her hand, in her hair, in her neck, and on her lips. He compared her to the sea, the heaven, the boats, to the clouds."[65] Goytisolo continues this stylistic device in *La resaca* and later novels also.

Of special interest in all these novels in his portrayal of Spanish reality is his concentration on the theme of death as a symbol of peace, as a means of evading reality, as a symbol of manliness, or as a reflection of the spiritual death Spain has apparently suffered and which events in his novels document. In *Juegos de manos, Duelo en el Paraíso,* and *El circo* the principal theme concerns a murder, although the criminals vary in age and social position. In *Duelo en el Paraíso* it is a group of young Basque refugee children at the end of the war; in *Juegos de manos* it is middle-class university students five years after the war; and in *El circo* the murderers belong to the lower middle class some ten years after the Civil War.

The groups, seeking their personal liberty, find it necessary to kill. Ana tells Mendoza in *Juegos de manos* that "I imagined then that all authentic men had to their credit at least one death."[66] David's reaction involves the maturing concept of the freedom of death as an evasion of reality. The adolescents of *Juegos de manos,* living in an empty, selfish world, have lost their innocence. The Davids representing a remnant of the idealism of the Spanish Republic cannot continue to live in a world where the Agustíns, the representatives of the Franco philosophy, dominate. Yet as Agustín implies, by killing David he and his kind kill themselves and thus expiate their guilt. Then, too, death may bring the only available peace in Spain. "His face expressed a great peace, as Agustín had never seen on him in his life."[67]

The boys in *Duelo en el Paraíso*, because of their youth, may not know what they do, and thus for them, as has already been shown, the future supposedly holds some hope. Yet Pablo, who with his young companions robbed slain citizens of their possessions, "was convinced that no boy could become an adult if he did not have to his credit at least one death."[68] Death may come in poetic form. "The Archangel, his dream converted into reality, arranged his arms and legs like those of the children of the story, and put a bundle of flowers on his breast."[69]

For Utah of *El circo* life is absurd anyway, and he is quite willing to accept responsibility for a murder he did not commit. For others in *El circo*, to kill is to get ahead and preserve oneself. "The first moment of fear having passed, he felt stronger and more sure of himself. In the future he would have money to display."[70]

The murder with the most obvious perverse overtones is that of Pira in *Fiestas*. Yet it is the one which is described in the most poetic terms. "From far off, a bloody shred of her blouse seemed to float among her fingers like a delicate bouquet, the delicate bouquet of flowers she had dreamed of presenting to the Pope."[71]

Eugenio de Nora states: "In any of these works we find fragmentarily, traits of the true novelist—in the focus of the theme, in the conception, presentation and movement of the situations, in the supposed ideology . . . in the rhythm with which the action develops and bursts forth—; but beside these evident values and findings, the errors, the expressive deficiency, at times including the unjustified and almost unexplainable eruption of the gratuitous and easy topic, undermine more or less gravely, the final impression."[72] Such an appraisal from a critic accepted by the Establishment may be suspect, for one must concede that these early novels gave Goytisolo a name as the most powerful novelistic voice of his generation and the first internationally known Spanish novelist since Camilo José Cela.

CHAPTER 4

The Later Novels (1958-1966)

I *The Undertow (La resaca), 1958*

THE CHURCH is planning a great holiday in honor of the
Virgin. Antonio, bored by his family, joins a gang of juvenile
delinquents and helps exploit the Church's drive for funds for
the religious festival in order to obtain money for himself and
the gang, especially for its leader, Metralla, whom he dreams
of accompanying to America. The wife of an image maker who
had lost her own son pays Antonio's family so that he will come
and live with her, a deception Metralla encourages, for he wants
Antonio to steal her money. Antonio does so. Metralla, in turn,
absconds with the money. Coral, a young prostitute whose own
father had raped her, enjoys doll collecting and lives with the
gang. She introduces Antonio to sex during the festival of San
Juan, when he becomes drunk. She eventually ends up in a re-
formatory. Antonio's drunken father, Cinco Duros, blackmailed
by his own sons, Antonio's brothers, spends his time with his
friend and drinking companion, Cien Gramos, with whom he
alternately argues, fights, and becomes reconciled.

Saturio is a great ally of the Church, but his daughter is
accidentally poisoned, and he becomes extremely bitter, broods,
and gets drunk every day. His son, Carlitos, is chosen to make
a speech of welcome to the Church Delegate, but overcome by
the situation in which they live, he can only babble, "we are
poor . . . my father," as the authorities of the festival pass in
front of a somewhat indifferent crowd, to flag waving and
marching music.

Giner, a Republican, has suffered for his beliefs. Neither his extremely religious wife nor his children love or respect him. He hopes for activity of some kind which will bring the worker a measure of dignity, but he is arrested. His friend, Emilio, the labor organizer, says that only in France can one live and work. Evaristo, an old war veteran, in spite of the omnipresent government signs, "not a home without light, nor a Spaniard without bread," is dispossessed of his house, and commits suicide.

As we have seen, according to the author this documentary novel introduces a new dimension to his work. First announced under the title of *Los murcianos*, and banned in Spain, it treats life in a Barcelonian suburb. Goytisolo said that he discovered in Barcelona a life he did not know existed because of his own protected childhood, and in the violent shock of discovery, *La resaca* was born. (He was later to fuse this documentary type of novel with a special kind of travel literature.) He abandons the autobiography found in earlier works. He says: "In reality I did not know anything beyond my social milieu before I wrote *La resaca*."[1] He saw in this novel a presentation of facts directly communicated through the characters, as he tried to abandon fantasy and poetry for a photographic reality of frustrated victims of a society who try to forget in drink their despair and defeat. He wanted to offer no judgment but rather a simple and implacable photography which seems to deny the hope offered by Antonio Machado (*La resaca* is the third part of the trilogy based on "The Ephemeral Tomorrow").

> But another Spain is born
> the Spain of the chisel and the mace
> with that eternal youth which is formed
> from the solid past of the race.
> An implacable and redeeming Spain,
> Spain which dawns
> with an ax in her avenging hand,
> Spain of anger and ideas.[2]

One will recall that Goytisolo rejected the objectivist novel as postulated by Robbe-Grillet. The latter recognized that the novel concerns the experience of both author and reader, but he viewed the novel itself as an isolated object, a statement of its own reality. The author had to remove his own feelings and give free rein to the reader's imagination. In his description of his technique in *La resaca,* Goytisolo comes close to following the objectivists, in spite of his refutation, but he knows that to render an "impermeable world" is impossible. Thus he combines his observation as a painter with an imagination a true objectivist would not use. His social conscience also refutes his objectivism. Although, ironically, he tries to use Ortega's definition given in *The Dehumanization of Art* to maintain a maximum distance from his subjects and to allow himself the minimum amount of sentimental intervention, one senses that the isolation of the characters represents his own isolation, their loss of idealism, his own frustration.

La resaca involves a camera technique and time experimentation and domination we have encountered previously, as well as focus-shifts from character to character and generational associations.

Stretched out on the bed she watched her leave. Suddenly, without knowing why, she saw her again, two years before, more robust, younger, bent over her, shrieking. Coral was then a skinny, little, but well developed girl. Her grandmother had given her a showy dress, and she showed herself with it throughout the district, her hair adorned with flowers. Whenever the music sounded, her feet, as though drawn by a puppeteer, wanted to dance. Disguised, she ran after gypsies, organ grinders, guitarists . . . One day, on entering her hut, she found a man whom she did not know. Crying, her grandmother explained that it was her father.[3]

Goytisolo uses these time stops to further the plot, to explain character relationship, and to involve the reader, rather than to offer a development, chronological or fragmentary, of his characters' experiences as individuals.

They kept advancing, advancing toward him, and a terrible anguish entered his throat. Perched on the roof of a hut, Hombre-Gato and Ramón laughed and made obscene gestures with their hands. And suddenly, like a condemned man about to die, his life passed nakedly before his eyes, and he recalled Saturio and the little girl, Giner and the old man thrown out of his home. Uncontainable tears burst forth, obscuring his vision of the smiling and benign group, and when the music stilled and the priest signalled him with his arm, he could only babble: "Delegate . . . We are poor . . . My father . . ."[4]

Each chapter within the seven larger sections of *La resaca* centers the action around one character, although other plot threads are alluded to and interwoven. Thus the first chapter concerns Antonio, although it sets the stage for Saturio and the celebration to take place within a few weeks. The second chapter involves Giner and his circumstances, while introducing Emilio, Cien Gramos, and Cinco Duros. Chapter three returns to Antonio, and introduces the new element of the wife of the image maker and Metralla's gang. The next chapter refocuses on Giner, and builds the suspense about Emilio and his letter. The fifth chapter deals with Giner's companions; the following one portrays Saturio and his family. Each of the chapters leaves the reader on a rising inflection of suspense. Chapter one ends with Antonio's search; the next one with an invitation by Cien Gramos to have a drinking bout; the third one involves an invitation to Antonio to join the gang; the next chapter ends as Giner opens Emilio's letter. The second section continues with an intensification of the plot elements, and each chapter within it alternates and refocuses as before on the various characters and their existence. Antonio practices his apprenticeship. Giner's beliefs are reinforced by Emilio's letter. Plans for the Religious Congress accelerate. In the third section, Giner meets Emilio. Each sub-chapter again stops somewhat abruptly without resolution, increasing reader interest in the denouement. In the fourth section, and in the following ones, resolution of previous plot threads occurs. Antonio learns about sex, and Saturio's child dies; in the fifth section Antonio confesses his theft to the woman, is betrayed by Metralla, and abandons his childhood; in the sixth section Evaristo commits suicide; and the final section ends with the religious activities of the Sunday, the culmination of the festival which is the unifying theme through all the sections. The seventh section ends on a Sunday, just as the first one had begun on a Sunday.

La resaca is probably Goytisolo's most brutal novel. The title implies that the undertow or surf tosses up an odd and often evil-smelling brew which comprises the Spain of the post-Civil War period. The work is filled with prostitutes, the usual homosexual, beggars, and buyers of stolen goods, each with his special vocabulary or thieves' cant. Goytisolo includes a special glossary of terms at the end of his novel to enlighten the reader, for he uses his language to convey perceptions and emotions too heavy for a unilinear prose. As the author examines the daily reality, the reader may postulate the possibility of another reality which ought to exist but which is as unreal as the grotesque one portrayed. Goytisolo uses a variety of other techniques in his reproduction of his social reality, but here his technical ability seems of secondary importance.

The criminals and outcasts are victims of the atmosphere in which they have been brought up. Antonio realizes that only in his identification with the gang can he achieve a sense of meaning in life, to escape his feeling of being a poor child from a district of shacks, to be known for himself and not as the son of Cinco Duros who is constantly drunk in Maño's tavern. With the band, as one of its members, he feels himself to be strong and feared, a real man. The newspapers constantly refer to incidents such as: "The aggressors formed a band of little thieves, social dregs, formed almost in its majority by adolescents, which like a plague, falls at any given moment on the business enterprises of the city, making them victims of their thievery and of their capricious tributes."[5] For the younger generation, however, criminals such as Francisco Martín Sabater, alias "el Quico," are heroes. As Metralla points out, "A guy like that is a real man . . . All those who were like him [brave] were liquidated."[6] During the War he was a valiant fighter. The youngsters feel that brave deeds were possible during that period, but that now, the only heroes and ones without fear are the criminals and rebels against society. Antonio, for one, always felt cheated when the boys talked of the War. He thought that destiny had played him an evil trick, for he had been born into a sterile society where acts of heroism were rare. Even though the papers spoke of constant violence, robbery, and murders, he saw himself hemmed in by the monotony and mediocrity of his present life which caused him both to pity and scorn himself.

Against a background in which the children accepted as natural a life in which parents were hanged and where torture and murder were everyday occurrences, the Church, the central protagonist and also antagonist in many of Goytisolo's novels, fails to live up to its responsibilities. It exacts donations from the faithful. Clerics tell the poor that man does not live by bread alone, and they should not think of material things. The sweet, suave voice of the Church advertises: "A great Marian concentration took place today, at the venerated image of Our Lady of Fatima, as a spiritual preparation for the Holy Week."[7] As part of the great Church Easter Festival, the children of the good Christian families take communion. The poor ones come for the clothes they may receive. A catechist passes out reading material and tells them to read it at home. The children explain that they cannot read. The catechist tells them to deliver the material to their parents. When Hombre-Gato tells him that his father cannot read either, the representative tells him: "Well. In this case . . . The young man interrupted himself, cut short. In this case. His inspiration failed him again and he concluded rapidly. Circulate . . . Work. Circulate . . . Hombre-Gato settled into his chair, triumphantly. The children formed a compact block in front of the varnished desk of the priest. On the stand there was a wooden crucifix and the portraits of Franco and José Antonio. At the foot someone had written a caption: 'Man does not live by bread alone. Our rule is not materialistic.' "[8] The Church's support of the oppressive regime reinforces the hypocrisy of the latter's slogan in the district, "Not a house without light, nor a Spaniard without bread." The Church tells the laboring classes that they will bring a kingdom of peace through their nobility and through the blood of their children and their children's children and their victorious struggle for order and social justice. The struggle will be difficult, but strong men are ready to undertake it as they and their parents did in the trenches. Wildly applauded, the Delegate pronounces the ritual invocations as the National Hymn plays. Somewhat sadly Goytisolo must admit that the people find consolation in the immunity to change of the Church, their one security in a time of disintegrating society.

As the Church Delegate speaks on the radio, Giner and his friend discuss similar matters in the cafe. Goytisolo employs their discussion as the counterpoint melody to the Church activities. Giner, the poor garage worker, and thousands like him, came from the South to live and die in a society where the poor sell their children for money to buy food for the rest of the

family. He fluctuates between hope and despair. He knows that
in Spain all men are slaves, but he feels that men should be
willing to act for future freedom and liberty, even though they
know their sacrifice will have no immediate results.

"We all desire justice, but we shall never obtain it, if we do not
demand it now, when, on doing so, we know that they will not want
to listen to us . . . To reclaim liberty, we cannot wait until the moment
in which our claim is practical since, to make it possible one day,
we must ask for it now, when it is still utopian . . . Everything . . . My
failure and yours . . . The First Republic was a utopian undertaking
and the Second also . . . I understood it suddenly: everything had
been until now impossible and, in spite of it, necessary. And I knew
that we could not renounce utopia because, thanks to our previous
failures and our coming failures, the Republic would arrive one day
and this time would be viable."[9]

Goytisolo's constant theme is modern man, and especially
Spanish man, on whom he focuses with great intensity. The Spain
in which he lives, as Goytisolo depicts it, is truly degenerate.
"The boy sat down on a pile of rubbish, his back to the sun. At
his side, an old man dressed in a filthy overcoat was cutting his
toe nails. Two beggars poked through the garbage with sticks."[10]

Slowly, with his penis out, he aimed at Jarque's house, and in front
of everybody began to urinate against the wall. . . . Antonio followed
the trajectory of his arm with a mixture of fascination and horror.
Metralla had seized his rival by the neck and was beating his head
against the cobblestones. Jarque's convulsed face, splattered with
bruises, didn't seem to invoke any pity in Metralla. Jarque's efforts to
free himself became weaker and more infrequent. Suddenly Metralla
snatched a stone and smashed it several times against his face.
  Antonio closed his eyes and opened them again. Jarque had his
forehead split open and his mouth full of blood. Astride his abdomen
Metralla watched him, his face streaming sweat. The boys in the gang
asked for more, more, shouting. To please them, he dragged the inert
body to the bank and thrust its head into the water.
  Immediately, the hysteria of his buddies reached its peak. As though
moved by a spring, they bent over the body of the victim and began
to shower blows and kicks on him.[11]

"The zone had become converted into a giant dung heap and
dozens of hungry dogs wandered through the garbage."[12] "A

man wounded his wife seriously with a knife and another beat his son with a hammer. The Press of the city took note of the incidents and *La Vanguardia* published an article of an eminent sociologist on 'the low index of morality of the less favored classes.' "13

Antonio earned more in a day without working than his father earned in a week of breaking his back. He had gone to the Hideout, knowing that one less mouth to feed in the house would help all concerned, and when he saw his mother, he gave her all the money he had with him, feeling both scorn and pity. The conclusion of Antonio and his friends is that words such as "bread," "justice," "man" have lost significance and serve only to promote the big lie of a hypocritical Church and an oppressive and deceitful government. False friends, indifferent children, and criminal delinquents, themselves victims of the system, live out hopeless lives, escaping temporarily through sensuality or hostility. The young men feel they will be nothing in their lifetime "Honor does not work in this country," the professor had told Antonio. "Here, he who does not steal, bites his fists with hunger."14 And Antonio, realizing that the world is one giant enterprise of exploitation, decides he is not going to be the one to pull the chestnuts from the fire for a handful of rascals.

Each victim meets his boundary situation in a different way. Evaristo finds that true rebellion is impossible, and dispossessed and disinherited, he commits suicide, dying with his eyes fixed on the optimistic and hypocritical government sign about light and bread for the Spanish home. Antonio finds temporary identification with his anti-social gang, but he finally understands with a mixture of sadness and relief, that his childhood is dead and that he will not be able in the future to escape from himself and his responsibilities. Saturio turns to drink. Giner dreams of utopia. Indeed, much of the novel may be viewed as a dream state, for almost nothing is certain. The talk about America is not necessarily real, and we can never be sure of Metralla's betrayal. In what seems to be a dream sequence one may infer that Antonio, in part, is no longer a child because of his sexual entanglement with the image maker's wife.

Using a third person narrative and an abundance of dialogue

with almost dramatic intensity at times, Goytisolo attempts to achieve the objectivity and omniscience of an author not involved in the action, simply telling and showing us what is occurring in the characters' everyday life in all its exciting and unexciting details. Nevertheless, although Goytisolo describes events without commentary so the reader may decide for himself, and although the camera eye shows the varying situations and viewpoints of all the characters, one is forced to conclude that little hope, if any, exists in Spain. This is, of course, Goytisolo's own viewpoint. The picture he presents is so negative that it is difficult to hope for the future. One ray of light may lie in Antonio's maturation and in Giner's dreams for the future, in spite of his wife's hostility and his children's indifference. At the very least Antonio will survive, something David could not do. Through a new understanding of the need for love and dignity among the abandoned and unloved, he may break the pattern of Spanish fear and complacency, a pattern which attempts to ruin Giner and all others who seek to maintain integrity in their society; but the reader's reaction to Goytisolo's identification with the best of human aspiration, if that is what it is, is that the wicked world will always frustrate the noble and the ideal.

The events of the middle 1960's in Spain show the growing rebellion of Spanish youth and university students against Franco's oppressive regime and an increasing demand for a democratic Spain, but *La resaca* reveals no new picture of hope which events may have brought to Spain, making the so-called objective reality a grotesque one. Goytisolo was attempting to paint a reality, sure that real history and developing events would not prove him to be unprophetic. Perhaps Goytisolo does not put social values ahead of literary ones, but it is equally true that he feels literature cannot be divorced from life. Thus Giner and the other characters to whom nothing extraordinary or special happens, seem largely social types who serve as man's indictment of society. Nevertheless, as literature, *La resaca's* individual structural bricks contribute to the composition of a coherent and meaningful novel, for we are fully aware that what we are reading is just that and not simply a sociological report.

II *The Island* (*La isla*), 1961

Claudia Estrada returns from abroad to Torremolinos, near the coast of Málaga, after an absence of six years, to spend a vacation with her husband Rafael, newspaper writer and government official. The couple, no longer in the first bloom of youth, have not lived together for a long time and have drawn apart spiritually, emotionally, and physically. Rafael's parents belong to the middle class. He and Claudia, an ex-Falangist worker, have lost their political illusions, becoming both cynical and indifferent. On her return she discovers that Málaga and the surrounding country have changed considerably during her absence. They have become pleasure areas for rich Spaniards and foreigners, especially Americans, whose manners the rich Spaniards seek to ape. They and their companions indulge in constant drinking and debauchery. Claudia gradually becomes a part of the gross materialistic world of animal instincts. At the first party she attends, a woman fetes all her previous lovers, and her husband pays the bills. Miguel and Magda have a miserable marriage. Laura sleeps with everyone. Claudia knows that misery and poverty abound, but hunger and deprivations are not words for the tourists. Gregorio deceives his wife with an American girl but resents attentions given his own wife. Román seeks love affairs everywhere, to the pretended indifference of his actress wife, Dolores Vélez, who feels she is becoming too old for him. Rafael's mistress is a French model who in turn has a lover, an Italian aristocrat. Rafael's excessive drinking and skirt chasing have finally caused the displeasure of his superiors at the Ministry. Claudia herself loves the impotent Enrique. After eleven dizzy days Claudia leaves, realizing that time is passing her and Spain by, and that the spiritual and physical erosion will continue. The unhappy Dolores keeps Román, and Claudia remains with Rafael for the sake of his career.

La isla was published originally in French as *Chronique d'une île* in 1961. Subsequently, that same year, the Spanish edition appeared. Goytisolo no longer treats the Spanish child or adolescent, except peripherally, as with Claudia's nephews. The Civil War youngsters have now grown up, but the picture, if possible, is even grimmer than before, as the title implies, for Torremolinos is the microcosm which represents all of Spain. "It has changed, hasn't it? It was an idle question and I limited myself to nodding my head. Well, wait until you meet the people. It has been converted into a country apart, into a real island . . . Husbands deceive their women. Women deceive their husbands. The priest threatens and nobody pays any attention to him. Virginity has disappeared from the map and all men are fairies."[15]

The constant emphasis is on Spanish sensuality and sexuality, which overshadows every aspect of the character's lives. The taxi driver, accustomed to the easy virtue of most of his fares—one out of every two passengers, he says—invites Claudia to come to a hotel with him. He explains that he likes experienced ladies and that as a gentleman he likes to give them pleasure, even though in his district there is a fifteen-year-old girl who is just dying to go to bed with him. He is willing to believe that Claudia is refusing his offer only because she already has a boy friend. As he explains, "The foreign women have us badly accustomed . . . They come here only for this and one becomes overconfident, and, at times, he makes a mistake."[16] The selfishness, infidelity, and dissipation of the Spaniards are performed in an almost mechanical and lackadaisical manner, a reflection of their meaningless and boring life. They suffer from abulia; they are moral cowards unable to act positively, victims, in a sense, of the hopeless environment, as they seek to avoid the agonies of the political and sociological reality of modern Spain.

The wealthy tourists, foreigners in general, and Spaniards have helped contaminate Spain with their *dolce vita*, and destroy Spain's old sense of honor. Now a Spaniard, for twenty dollars, says one of the characters, might denounce his own father. The Americans, with their pink blank faces, are interested mainly in whiskey. Miss Bentley is interested in gypsy dances. Betty, the seventy-year-old nymphomaniac, and Ellen, Gerald's wife, have affairs by the hundreds. The Spaniards' imitation, even of this alien dissipation, is artificial and badly done. As Claudia tells Gregorio, pained at his wife's infidelity, "You want to imitate the Americans and you imitate them badly. To live like them . . . one has to wear his horns gracefully."[17] Miss Bentley, whose

GOYTISOLO

family in America was extremely wealthy, lived in a madcap manner. She and others like her helped destroy Spanish individuality and create a completely cynical and materialistic world, where everything is done for money. Dolores exclaims: "You are rich and in Spain, we adore rich Americans. Yes, indeed: if you should lose half your money, we would love you half as much. And if you had only a third, a third. And if you had nothing . . ."[18] Yet these cynical, tragic twentieth-century Spaniards are human beings who would welcome real feeling in a loveless land of lesbians, homosexuals, drunkards, idlers, and adulterers. Surrounded by sexual abnormalities, living a solitary life empty of purpose, the characters only occasionally reveal their human potential. Goytisolo seems to imply that beneath the surface there may still be a real Spain, one which must resist the corruption which has come to her shores. Some hope may yet remain for the adolescents of *Juegos de manos*, as unhappy as adults in *La isla* as they were as adolescents, but it is a faint one.

Claudia recalls her altruism of the past which now causes her to laugh. When she was eighteen she had imagined that existence was a gift of great value and that the world could be changed. She recalled how her parents were executed one morning without her being able to kiss them good-bye. She had felt for a time she was fighting for a noble cause, realizing only little by little what the world was really like. The easy romanticism of the War years disappeared. The War had not really changed anything. The rich came out of hiding, and Spain became its own worst enemy again, as she and other Spaniards showed themselves as selfish, scornful, cynical, and intolerant. It was necessary to keep on making the sacrifices and gestures of the preceding years, as though some miracle would occur, but none came to pass, and Claudia eventually stopped believing. By the time Rafael was transferred to Madrid, nothing remained in her soul of her earlier enthusiasm, love of her fellow man or a general idealism.

Claudia's eleven-day trip to Torremolinos, a symbolic voyage to recover, if possible, the illusions of the past, political as well as personal, was doomed to failure from the moment of its inception. On her arrival she buys a cornucopia of peanuts be-

[88]

cause she recalls her walks with Rafael. She slips back, almost immediately, into the local accent, and feels her heart quicken with happiness. Everything that assails her senses carries her back to her childhood, or to her life with Rafael. The taxi she takes is a Peugeot, a kind of car that Rafael used to drive. She soon realizes that everything is different, that the idyllic Torremolinos of her youth has cracked open like a soap figurine. She feels as though time has died, for the years succeed each other uselessly. At novel's end Claudia can only say, "Time went fast and the erosion continued."

Claudia's relationship to Enrique recalls a similar relationship between Jake Barnes and Brett Ashley in Hemingway's *The Sun Also Rises*. Love is possible only for two people who are incapable of full expression of that love. Jake was made impotent by a war wound on the Italian front (an exact parallel may be found in the experience of Jordi in *Duelo en el Paraíso*). In *La isla* Enrique is also impotent. Both women want and yet can't stand their lover's touch which turns them to jelly. The men angrily, if briefly, turn against the women, who feel or are made to feel like whores. Claudia's frustration, on a personal level, complements her ideological frustration. The atmosphere of both novels is that of a war-wearied lost generation which seeks love affairs, drink, and new sensations. Both novels are set in Spain. Both are written in the first person, with Jake and Claudia as narrators respectively.

The physical aspects of the post-War years are as unattractive as the human ones. Enrique Olmos writes Claudia that every day the odor of gas and oil grows stronger, everything is noisier, and there are more police. Progress has brought damaging changes. He used to be able to swim in the river, a magnificent river. Although it is still there, they can no longer swim in it, for its surface is covered with grease and waste materials from the industries along its shores. Simple pleasures have been replaced by the sophisticated ones found in elegant clubs where one can play bridge or tennis, consume whiskies and canapés in progressive and civilized fashion. Beneath this veneer of tourism and luxury lie great misery and poverty.

The historical reality, seen from another point of view, bears witness to the indefinable malaise of which Goytisolo speaks in his novel, and shows how contemporary events are illuminated by the past.

The casual visitor, however, will see little of this. It is largely hidden. In 1964 alone, 14 million tourists poured into Spain, seeking the long, lovely beaches, or camping by the sea in the colorful camp grounds that dot the coasts. Most come away enchanted. The roads of Spain, though bad, are improving; gasoline is abundant; new hotels, villas and pensions are springing up everywhere. Suspicion of the foreigner has given way to the jingle of the cash box, and tourism has become Spain's main industry, bringing half a billion dollars yearly to the coffers of a nation that six years ago stood on the brink of bankruptcy.[19]

As Goytisolo describes the landscape, he combines a sense of poetry and reality to show us both Spains.

At San Pedro de Alcántara, Dolores turned on to a narrow, steep highway full of ruts, and the panorama underwent a sudden transformation. We had left the ornamentation of the coast behind—the foreign cars, the bars, the billboards written in English—and we were going through Andalusia again, across a sunny and disagreeable perspective. The road wound up the sides of the mountain, and as the height increased, it seemed to me that one could breathe more easily. Enrique's automobile had lost its head start. The sun dressed it with fire in the distance, and at every turn he sounded his horn. The highway wound around the precipice. The pines grew down the crags of the slope and, after a level bit, the road entered the outskirts of a town. We met an army truck and a Seat with an official license. The mountains multiplied the echo of the horns. The Spanish firs mingled with the pines on the yellowish slopes. Dolores drove without saying anything. The sun lay in ambush at the turn of the curves, and constantly, she was obliged to brake. When we passed near a drink stand, the waitress and the soldiers waved at us. The vegetation decreased little by little. At a thousand meters, the highway was still climbing, and the last firs clutched the mountainside. Then the countryside lay completely bare. The bare peaks succeeded one another until they were lost from view, and for a few moments, not a tree was seen.[20]

According to Maurice Coindreau in the preface to the French editon, the heroine of the novel, and in a sense the voice of the author, is Dolores Vélez, the mysterious and tragic actress who feels that the social parasites of which Spain is composed have not suffered enough. She contends that if one could remove Spain's sunshine, women, and bull fights, Spaniards might learn more of life as it really is. She hates the "infected bourgeoisie." Yet it is Claudia, the protagonist, who gives us an almost hour-by-hour and day-by-day recital of the events of the eleven days from her viewpoint, which would make her Goytisolo's voice, thereby destroying the photographic reproduction of reality for which the author is striving.

Goytisolo has once more given us a spiritual and physical reproduction of a country without a soul, an accurate portrait of self-destructive hedonism in self-righteous Spanish society to which he had entry. Nora likes *La isla* for its psychological realism and critical intention.[21] Coindreau admits that Goytisolo has given us a novel of a life without spirit, without a heart, a life of eternal whiskies and abnormal sexuality. While he claims that Goytisolo is as much a memorialist as a novelist, he finds too much sunshine in his pen for him to paint what he terms a "flagellating picture," and further states: "In this work, a clever utilization of the resources of suggestion makes of this chronicle much more than a document valuable for the history of the customs of today. It is a work of an artist as much as it is of a memorialist. The testimony will perhaps lose its actuality, but the art of the novelist will remain, and it is one of the finest kinds in its savory variety."[22]

In spite of Coindreau's assertions, on reading Goytisolo's novels one may reach the easy conclusion that all Spaniards are debased, degenerate, and depraved, or engaged in a hopeless struggle for spiritual and physical survival in a hopeless land. Rafael's parents had been close to death during the Civil War, but they and others like them had learned nothing from their experience. If the Spaniard's alienation from the world of the spirit is as complete as Goytisolo pictures it to be, little purpose can be achieved in documenting it, for no one can breathe life into a corpse. It is perhaps on these grounds, as well as for the political implications, that many Spanish critics reject Goytisolo's novel rather than for purely literary reasons.

III *Holiday's End* (*Fin de fiesta*), 1962

Although the setting of the four short novels or long short stories, labeled simply Primera, Segunda, Tercera, and Cuarta (First, Second, Third, and Fourth), is Spanish, the problems examined might occur anywhere. With one exception no obvious political or national implications exist. Goytisolo examines marital relationships from four different points of view, that of the husband, that of the wife, and that of some outsiders. The stories move slowly in their descriptions of the psychological states of the people, their activities, and the countryside. The characters, as they experience their psychological travail in an attempt to find themselves, smoke, dance, sleep, hunt, fish, talk, and visit friends. As average activities of human beings, the unimportant quotidian pursuits reflect their boredom, but add a dimension of realism in the realization that they represent our own behavior. More realistically, and to a lesser degree, the types he presents represent the sensually motivated, although not abnormal, people he showed us in *La isla*, bored with life, with their families, and with themselves.

The first story concerns a Swedish couple who visit a small village in southern Spain. They indulge in sporadic drinking, quarreling, and reconciliation. The young narrator's friend Ramón, whose boat the couple hires, has a brief relationship with the wife. The husband unsuccessfully attempts suicide.

The second incident studies another psychological problem. Alvaro is flattered by the attentions of an adoring young girl, Loles, who also greatly admires his wife, Ana. The latter has several sophisticated friends, one of whom, Paco, falls in love with her. Ana is disturbed by Alvaro's seriousness, his indifference to her friends, and his possible affair with Loles. She realizes eventually that he is slowing down because he is becoming older, and finally reconciled to her situation, she becomes aware that she, also, is no longer young.

In the third selection Juan, a rich and rather spoiled architect, and his wife take a summer vacation. She and Jaime, one of Juan's friends, had had a brief affair, but she had told her husband about it when she realized that she truly loved him and not Jaime. Since that time Juan has embittered his own life and hers with his jealousy. Isabelo, a fisherman whose boat they hire, seduces a young Portuguese girl. Juan leaves his wife with Isabelo, but nothing happens. Juan finally works out his problems and realizes that his wife loves him.

The fourth incident relates Bruno's visit to his childhood friend, Miguel. When Bruno's father had died, Miguel's mother had invited him to spend the summer with them, and he had in time become almost a member of the family. Bruno, a Don Juan type with a French mistress, has a temporary affair with Gloria, whom he had known in France. Mara, Miguel's wife, quarrels with her husband constantly, for he has rejected several splendid teaching positions, has become moody, and has lost his capacity to enjoy life. He cannot accept the responsibilities his writing fame has brought him. He seeks his sole strength and support from his wife's presence, nevertheless. Mara enlists Bruno's aid in reawakening Miguel's interest in the world about him, for she loves her husband. Bruno, incidentally, tries to make love to Mara, but as he prepares to leave for France, he realizes his own and man's helplessness in the face of life's problems.

Basically the four stories are one. They examine the crisis in the relationships between a man and his wife, a situation into which a third person enters to give it added form and meaning but not a solution. In spite of the apparent insignificance of the incidents, Goytisolo's evocative power makes each reader feel potentially involved. The author conveys also a sense of the disproportion between man and a universe which is completely insensitive and wholly indifferent to him as an individual. As Alvaro says: "We pass our life speaking of unrealizable things. One day, we shall die intoxicated with words,"[23] and Miguel feels there is no cure for his loss of identity with people, the universe, or a joy in life.

Although Goytisolo's work concerns human relationships, the trials and tribulations of young and old, married and single, who seek companionship, understanding, and love, one glimpse of the political situation intrudes. "The television program had ended and, on the screen, there was a display of tanks and flags. One after another the image of the chiefs of the Movement advanced, growing larger toward the spectator, until it culminated in the serene and grave image of the Chief, while the emblems of Victory waved in the background and the sonorous band played the National Hymn."[24]

As in his other novels Goytisolo intersperses nature descriptions.

On leaving Barcelona the sky had clouded over; then it had grown clear once more and, now, the sun shone again between the eucalyptus branches. The frogs were croaking in the pool and I stopped to admire the view from the summer house. It was a landscape that I knew well and, full of joy, I found that it was as I remembered it. The hills grew gradually smaller in the direction of the coast, covered with carob trees and vines. The green of the pines was mixed with the yellow of the wheat fields and, farther on, sky and sea were confused in an imprecise blue fringe.[25]

Goytisolo often uses memory recall. This combined with a slowing and domination of time to help fill each individual hour with small remembrances, evinces a continuing love and nostalgia for his country which some feel he criticizes so unmercifully. "The festival brought an infinitude of memories back. Under the arcades there swirled a compact humanity of women wearing little paper hats and men in shirt sleeves, sweaty and lustful. The boys ran around with rattles, whistles and little horns. Some ran up to the girls and threw firecrackers at their legs. Everyone seemed possessed by the delirium of the noise. The rockets burst without interruption and even the automobile drivers who sought a place to park kept sounding their horns."[26]

This capacity for recall reveals his photographic eye, but it also shows his ability to combine nature descriptions with emotional and mental states.

The dogs were flushing out the rabbits and we heard them panting up the slope. Miguel walked at my side and, suddenly, he threw his gun to his shoulder and shot twice at a wild pigeon. The concussion left me deaf momentarily, and, as in my youth, I admired his sharp eye and the infallibility of his reflexes. The bird fluttered badly wounded. Luciano shot also but he missed. The pigeon kept on losing altitude and finally fell in the bush. And the dogs became tangled in the brambles looking for it . . .

Miguel wanted to collect the game and we entered the waterway.

The dogs tracked with their tongues out, following mysterious spoors. The heavy vegetation impeded our view and we climbed carelessly over the ploughed land toward the pine trees. There the landscape had changed a bit. The vines grew green on the slope covered with saplings. When the dogs cornered a rabbit we fanned out. José and Miguel ran up the hill and I heard several shots. It had been many years since I felt so happy. The medlar trees were beginning to ripen and the yellow of the wheat announced the nearness of the harvest. The frogs croaked in a nearby pond. I felt like shouting to Miguel that his despair was stupid and throwing myself down with him in the stubble to look at the cloudless sky and the birds flying back and forth overhead.[27]

Essentially Goytisolo presents largely inconclusive pictures of human relationships and the ambiguity of good and evil. *Primera* ends with the friend sad and old-looking. *Segunda* ends with the realization of both the husband and the wife that they are growing old and their need for reconciliation and understanding. *Tercera* shows us a contented husband who gives back the love letters which for him are no longer important. *Cuarta* reveals an understanding of man's unprotected role in life and the moral implications of existing in a complex world, as the party ends.

In spite of the ambiguity, more subtly than in his previous works, he has presented a decaying civilization, a spiritually empty and intellectually stagnant society where the future is dark and hopeless. For all the activity, the parties, and the wealth, do not disguise the futility of life in Spain, and each character fails, as his society has failed, through lack of manliness, through indifference to ideological considerations, through moral decay, and through inability to accept responsibility.

IV *Signs of Identity* (*Señas de identidad*), 1966

Alvaro Mendiola, a member of a conservative and socially prominent Barcelona family which had supported Franco in the Civil War, unable to accept their views went to France in October, 1952, on the pretext of studying cinematography. In so doing he abandoned his friends in the midst of a difficult fight for their political rights. In France he had worked sporadically on a sociological documentary about Spanish emigration and had indulged in political discussions in various cafes, especially that of Madame Berger where refugees gathered to plan reviews and political action which never materialized. Alvaro had tried to help the refugees at first but ended up by avoiding them completely. Engaging in his somewhat empty existence devoted largely to smoking, drinking, and getting through the day, he had met and fallen in love with Dolores, a girl who lived in his boarding house and whom he had helped out of a difficult financial situation. She had left her exiled Republican family in Mexico to travel and learn about a different kind of existence. Obtaining employment on a French newspaper, he traveled with her over the world. In early 1963 he suffered a heart attack, and fearing an approaching death, at the age of thirty-two he returned with Dolores to his family home near Barcelona five months later, in July. Dolores was concerned because of his excessive drinking.

As the story opens in August of 1963, Alvaro sits listening to Mozart's "Requiem" and looking through various family albums, photographs, and letters, indulging in a sentimental exploratory journey into his past, trying to discover who and what he really is, as he remembers the events of his life and those of his family and friends, in a series of temporal excursions to the past.

Two days earlier, Professor Ayuso, a liberal professor who had been imprisoned for two years and who had helped indoctrinate Alvaro and his friends with concern for the dignity of man, had died. Ayuso goes to an unmarked grave, its occupant still pursued even in death by the governmental "forces of order." A number of Alvaro's university friends attend the funeral. Alvaro recalls Antonio Ramírez Trueba, a native of Murcia, known at the university for his Marxist sympathies. After eighteen months in jail Ramírez had returned to his home town, patronized at first by the town's respectable society as the town "Communist," but he had been placed under severe restrictions when he insulted don Gonzalo, a conservative town leader, by refusing to associate with him. He had thus freed his soul, if not his body, through their enmity. Antonio had visited Dolores while Alvaro was in Cuba covering the Cuban revolution. Alvaro visits his cousin's former home in Cuba and has affairs and adventures with various young ladies. He recalls other university friends: Enrique, a Falangist who felt Franco had betrayed the revolution; Ricardo and Paco who led student demonstrations; and the strange, nihilistic Sergio, with whom he had visited the red-light district. Ana, Sergio's mother, wanting to share all his experiences, had had a relationship with him which bordered on the incestuous. She also had aroused Alvaro and almost become his lover. Later Alvaro visited the same scenes in Barcelona, after an absence of some seven years, to try and recover the emotions of the past. The setting had not changed, but he had. Sergio, abandoning his earlier bohemian ways, had become a successful businessman and had died in an automobile crash in 1955.

Alvaro had visited the cemetery where his own mother was buried, thus triggering memories of her funeral, his feelings at sixteen years of age, that if he did not cut his family ties he would end up buried and dissolved back into the elements, to share his family's absurdity forever.

One of his recollections concerns his father's assassination in 1936, which he had never been able to document fully. After the war his family, re-established in Barcelona, had also tried to find out the details. Alvaro journeyed to his father's grave to look up various people who might know something of the event. The Republic had tried to give the peasants work, but it was these same hungry peasants, victims of humiliations and injustices through the years, who had killed his father. Alvaro remembers his days as a refugee child and his quarrels with the French children.

He recalls his trips to various countries with Dolores, who had helped brighten his grey life, alleviating momentarily his anguish at his lost identity. In spite of his love for her, he had forced her to have an abortion, and for a brief period she had run off with Enrique to obtain revenge. After nine years they still love one another, in spite of various brief infidelities on his part, including a homosexual episode which reminded him of his adolescent love for Jerónimo López, one of the former family workers, hired while he was away at school. Alvaro's ultra-religious Aunt Mercedes suspected Jerónimo who, it developed, was a leader of the Maquis and had disappeared one day. Alvaro continues to recall hundreds of details and interwoven lives at various periods of his life, recent and remote, such as the visit of Ricardo and Artigas with two blond Danish pick-ups.

Alvaro remembers his grandmother and his visits to her garden, her later loss of memory, and his renewed visits after the Spanish Civil War, when she was living in an old folks' home. Through the pictorial record in the album, he revives the sugar mills and the slaves his great-grandparents had had in Cuba, and their descendants, useless and decorative parasites. He recalls the uniformly grey days at a religious school, which his respectable family had hoped would reintegrate him into the strict, unyielding, and dying moral code to which they subscribed. He recollects his even earlier religious exaltation and thoughts of childish martyrdom, encouraged by the vaguely remembered governess, Miss Lourdes. He conjures up his Uncle Eulogio with his youthful studies of astronomy, astrology, and the occult sciences and his enthusiasm for Spengler. He summons up once more the boarding house at which he had lived in France, at the home of a music teacher, Madame de Heredia, and her passionate love for Frederic who, rejecting her, had run off with her son.

The long vigil ends, and Alvaro, awake all night in his mental retrospection, leaves the sleeping Dolores to drive off, still tired, sick, and on the edge of suicide, to Barcelona, his native city.

Signs of Identity, Goytisolo's most outspoken attack on the Franco regime, presents biographies of birth and death, suffering and sorrow in the Spanish police state where, during twenty-five years of "peace," man had beaten, arrested, and killed defenseless fellow citizens for the crime of having defended their legal government, the Republic. No progress, says Goytisolo, will be able to wipe away the humiliations, the injustices, the persecution, the destroyed lives, of those years.

Goytisolo examines Spanish history from the 1930's on, the days of José Antonio Primo de Rivera, Ledesma, and others, recalling the public works programs, the depression, the Popular Front, the violence and unrest among starving peasants and their battles with the Civil Guard; he more forcefully condemns Franco for the spiritual and physical murder of his countrymen who are born, multiply, and die in silent resignation. Andalusia recalls a cemetery to him in its eternal misery: "A woman in mourning carried a jug on her head and even the mangy dog swatting flies with his tail seemed an exact replica of others seen a thousand times in a Southern town. On the edge of the cemetery the huts proliferated like a narrow harvest of mushrooms. You began to count them (almost as one counts sheep), but boredom overcame you. One hundred, two hundred? From your observation post (or was it an effect of the light) the last hut became confused with the first funeral monuments, as if the frontier existing between the two worlds had been suddenly erased."[28]

While the government publishes glowing statistics of economic recovery and progress, aided by military discipline and millions of tourists who inject new blood into an old country, underneath the modernization and

the brilliant varnish of the numbers and the insolent unfolding of comparisons, lay a dark river bed of suffering, an immense sea where no ray of light had touched or ever would: a barefoot, empty-handed and broken life of millions and millions of countrymen, frustrated in their personal essence, relegated, humiliated, sold; a suffering mass of beings entering the world without apparent logic; an instrument of work with the figure of a man, subject to the laws of supply and demand like a poor and spent piece of merchandise. A sewer of injustices, offenses, illness, death, his pain distilled drop by drop in a coarse buried still, his castles of sand perpetually swept by time, his concealed and invisible work of tropical coral, the support and base for the lazy, futile life of the others, would they serve, at least, as fertilizer and ferment, food and sustenance? Those of whom the son of God had said: "you are the salt of the earth," would they fertilize some time the arid and ungrateful land of their severe and immortal Stepmother?[29]

In analyzing Spanish history, Goytisolo clearly shows why he had originally tentatively labeled this novel *Elegía cívica* (*Civic Elegy*) when he had published a fragment in *Cuadernos de Ruedo Ibérico*. It is a lament for a lost, confused, perplexed, dying civilization. He presents the Fascists who believe in *hispanidad*, the Christian mission of Spanish Catholicism, the menace of communism which seeks to undermine, serpent-wise, and inculcate boys of good families with its deadly virus against the "glorious peace" and public order brought by Franco. Through Alvaro's odyssey he recalls the sardonic voices of the past, represented by his aunts and uncle as they speak of events following the Civil War, their patriotism, hunger, the possibility of restoring the Bourbons, the hostility of nations toward Spain, the red subversion they saw menacing Spain from 1939 to 1944, the desire on the part of some to forgive and forget. Young Alvaro, indoctrinated, awaited in terror the triumph of the red hordes who would overrun Spain and kill everybody. He recalls his family support of Hitler and their fears at the Allied victory.

At eight, as a result of his visit to his grandmother, Alvaro realized that everything, including himself, was subject to biological change. His grandmother's lack of recognition seemed to deny his own remembered past as though it had never existed. Some years later, before entering the university, he had occasion to look into the family album, not to recover a lost time but in the hope of finding some indication for his future in an examination of his hated genealogical tree. He thinks briefly of destroying the records so that they too might disappear into the nothingness from which his ancestors had come and to which they rightfully had returned. Although he had managed to cut the ties to his inheritance, he had not been able to free himself, nor had any other member of his generation, from his country, his social class, or a family full of fanatics and psychopaths. Only by purging himself of this past evil, from his slave-trading grandfather through his fascist family, could he restore his youthful innocence.

Alvaro's search for himself complements Spain's search for herself, and Ayuso, representing faith in a better world, in death seemed to signify the destruction of all youthful illusions and the impossibility of change, for it was he who had said: "I don't mind dying, if I can see the fall of this Régime."[30] But his students will never see their ideals realized either. Only during one day did Alvaro and his countrymen experience the thrill of feeling free. In 1951, angry at high streetcar fares, the Spanish people went on strike, creating for many, in a country deprived during decades of the sharp and savage feeling liberty brings, one of the most beautiful days of their existence, but in the next twelve years no other such day appeared. Alvaro's family and their friends considered the strike a communist plot against public peace, order, and authority, a new and shameless red offensive against Spanish spirituality and the "holy Crusade" of the "peerless" Caudillo.

At the university, students discuss politics and the pressures of military groups and the "friends of Cardinal Spellman in the United States" against the Spanish people's bid for freedom. Alvaro and his school friends lament the economic misery of so many, dressed in ragged clothes, in their hovels on miserable streets. Visiting newsmen have their pictures destroyed by Spanish secret police who want to replace them with approved pictures of beautiful buildings and a peaceful, happy population.

Alvaro recalls the refugees cruelly deprived of their country by good smug citizens who prided themselves on saving the unity and independence of Spain, on their avenues, statues, ceremonies, and mausoleums, savoring their triumph on earth and hopeful, through solemn masses, of a future eternal happiness in heaven. In France and elsewhere Alvaro discovered many-layered generations of refugees, men who lived a life of illusion involving an unrealistic return to Spain, for them a lost paradise. Their set of passionate beliefs lacks meaning or utility for the transformation of their society, and their empty rhetoric leads Goytisolo to comment on the responsibilities of Spanish intellectuals, and the abandonment of religious and ethical value systems. At times, feeling themselves a trivial group on the periphery of life, the refugees escape into a world of sexual frenzy, populated by French and Danish nymphomaniacs. Many are complicated and tortured personalities. Those who return to Spain, with their German camera and their fantasies about their sexual adventures, are ready to reinforce concepts of Spanish manliness, and the superiority of the Spanish way of life. Political involvement, privation, hunger, injustice, and persecution are among the reasons for fleeing Spain. The groups themselves, in Madame Berger's cafe and elsewhere, spend their time arguing political action in common to avoid the constant internecine strife among them, a confusion symptomatic of lost souls trying to find a meaning in their actions. Parisian intellectuals meet with them and talk of revolution, but with the Algerian revolt, lose interest in Spain.

The documents Alvaro collects in order to reconstruct and synthesize bring back memories of dark and revealing facets of life in Spain, a series of biographies of citizens arrested for supposed communist activities, their beatings, jailings, and starving families. Many departed Spain to wander through Europe, while many stayed behind to pay with their lives for their attempts to transform Spain. Even more tragically, some who stayed behind had become inhibited and had grown old without having had any real purpose for living. Good middle-class citizens, repelled by the sight of poverty and dirty beggars after five centuries of conformity, respectably repudiated Christian morality.

Alvaro (and Goytisolo) arrive at 1963 in their spiritual odyssey and find a nation without a soul, living in a limbo of its own making, suffering unforgettable memories but with no real viable national purpose. The twenty-four years of peace imposed by Franco and his dogma, the spies, the censors, had instilled an intellectual conformity which rejected new ideas. Soon it would no longer be necessary to have secret police, for the dogma had become a part of the fabric of over thirty million Spaniards who welcomed the French, Swiss, Belgians, Dutch, Germans, English, Scandinavians, and Americans who came to see the bull fights, take the sun, and initiate the Spanish people into the indispensable exercise of industrial values. Sadly he reflects on the dead of the Spanish Civil War and his bitter generation, condemned to grow old without ever having been truly young nor yet having enjoyed freedom and responsibilty.

And so *Signs of Identity*, Goytisolo's most ambitious novel and perhaps his masterpiece, explores historical, geographical, temporal, and spatial relationships in a search for and an analysis of these signs and their meaning for the author. Goytisolo uses an almost geological superimposition of events to replace the linear progression one normally expects. Myth, psychology, poetry, objective and lyrical descriptions (a must in every Goytisolo novel) fuse with the situations and events he describes, as he employs every imaginable technique to further his aim: first, second, and third-person singular; first, second, and third-person plural; interior monologue; flashbacks; stream of consciousness; and rapidly shifting images and scenes. For the political and historical setting or its interpretation by his family, he employs the first-person plural. For his own recall he addresses himself in the second singular, but his personally interconnected relationships involving asides within a recollection, often shift from the second person to a third person and back to the second person to join all the elements of his review.

The first-person plural historical excursions involve no interior punctuation and use only beginning and ending quotation marks. In a shift from a recalled family oration to another historical event (still in his mind, but one step closer to consciousness and historical narrative), he uses dots, but the transition to the present is usually made without indicators except a sporadic use of additional spacing between paragraphs. Second-person interior monologues normally use quotation marks and punctuation, but not consistently, and a shift to these monologues may or may not be indicated. The three dots used at the beginning of the following sample are to indicate a fragment of a first-person monologue too long to give in its entirety; they are not a part of the original. Goytisolo, as previously indicated, uses no punctuation in passages of this nature.

. . . but hunger-misery mourning as in the years of red terror which some inveterately nostalgic people and dedicated delinquents wanted to restore for its profit and advantage opposed as they are to the growing interest of the free world in the progress and realities of a régime that has been and God willing will continue being the firmest bulwark of its security against Asiatic totalitarianism and its bold designs we let us repeat it once more we and in imitation of us all worthy citizens with Authority on the side of the law next to the providential Caudillo knowing perfectly the trick which is aired weapons on the arm as always in all the roads trenches and crossings

. . . Surprised also you attended astonished the violent awakening of your countrymen . . . in the middle of the street, under your own window, they were throwing rocks, throwing rocks at the streetcars.

The retinue went rapidly toward the exit of the cemetery . . .[31]

Following is a sample of second-person use in which Goytisolo has punctuation. The passage demonstrates also his use of tense shift.

Flatten with your foot the multiple holes of an antheap patiently con-
structed grain by grain on a pleasant sandy earth and come back the
next day: you will see again flourishing and subtle, like the modeling
of the gregarious instinct of its stubborn, laborious community, in the
same way the natural home of Spanish fauna, the ancestral and always
slandered hut of cane and tin, condemned to disappear, now that you
are, so to speak, Europeans and tourism obliges you to renew the
façade in the expedited and somewhat brutal manner, as one must
recognize, of modern and powerful organized neo-capitalism. . . .
You contemplated that kingdom of Taifa composed of huts and hovels
so similar to the one you filmed long ago (a kingdom destroyed after-
wards by decree with the solemn delivery of comfortable clean dwellings to its rough and suspicious inhabitants) and the indignation which
possessed you previously seemed as strange to you as . . .
      Richard had parked the Seat . . .[32]

Goytisolo often combines stream of consciousness and interior
monologue. "Sixth course of the baccalaureate, section B. Forty
adolescents dressed in golf pants, tie and hard collar, clustered
in compact files their backs to the pompous neo-Gothic windows
of the old school building. In a corner of the photograph, near
Alvaro, the severe and circumspect figure of the reverend father
confessor. 'Father, I accuse myself of having sinned three times
against the sixth commandment.' 'With thought or with actions,
my son' . . ." From the recalled confession of a masturbatory
incident he goes directly into the stream of consciousness. "Consequences physical and moral of the impure act. Classification
of celestial hierarchies with specific properties of each one of
them. Tesino, Trebia, Trasimeno, Canas, Pichincha, Chimborazo
and Cotopaxi. Binomium of Newton, oviparous, viviparous, ovi-
viviparous. Barbara, celare, darii, ferio. Formula for bicarbonate
of soda. Theorem of Pythagoras . . . Opportune and diaphanous
the chorus of the *Lacrimosa dies illa* . . ."[33] From the recalled
conversation with the priest he drifts directly into the subconscious and also into fragmented recall. To mark his return to the
present he again uses dots and noise, in this case music, to
return him to consciousness. Often, in giving the biographies or
case histories of the refugees, Goytisolo switches to italics, as
he does in the constant shift in one chapter from his own life
experiences to those of his friend, Antonio, to convey the presentation as coming from official police and newspaper sources.

[104]

Goytisolo shifts from past to present rapidly, moving also from past to a further past and then to a future, which is still past to the present. The entire three decades covered by the novel, in actual elapsed time, take one day. As Virginia Woolf stated: "The mind of man, moreover, works with equal strangeness upon the body of time. An hour, once it lodges in the queer element of the human spirit, may be stretched to fifty or a hundred times its clock length; on the other hand, an hour may be accurately represented by the time-piece of the mind by one second. This extraordinary discrepancy between time on the clock and time in the mind is less known than it should be and deserves fuller investigation."[34] Alvaro, recalling the details of his life, exhibits a certain inconsistency in remembering elapsed time, stating that he left Spain in 1952 and in 1953, that his heart attack was five months and six months earlier, and that Sergio had died in 1955 and in 1956.

Alvaro falls asleep in the garden but awakens to begin his extraordinary mental voyage. It is from this moment in time that he undertakes his major excursion, but he later will use other temporal points, within his major present framework, to travel to other past events. "You had been asleep and, on opening your eyes, you sat up. The clock said ten minutes of seven. . . You could drink a shot of Fefinanes, frozen and blond, just enough to wet your lips, but you couldn't decide. The clouds had cleared up during your sleep and the sun persisted in the inflamed twilight sky. But your tranquility had not been disturbed momentarily and, abandoning the garden, you could still, if you so desired, wander at your leisure near the pond, smell the dense perfume of the rosemary. . ."[35]

Instead he wonders what he might find if he went through letters of former family slaves, letters in French, his old school books. He felt he was living in a state of suspended animation without a real past or future and in an uncertain present. He decided to search in the old albums for the key to his childhood and youth, without hope, but fearing death. Thus as the afternoon waned, through interior monologue, stream of consciousness, and a series of flashbacks, he began his trip. Throughout, as in his other novels, the specific time within another temporal unit is important. "That night neither of you two had

slept. . . . At nine your mother had served your breakfast.
. . . That afternoon the tray . . . Miss Lourdes cried silently and
some days later. . . . While the war lasted, a refugee with your
mother and uncles and aunts in Southern France. . . . When the
Nationals won . . . From then on . . . The Spanish Civil War
had caught him in Havana and that same July 18 at seven sharp
in the evening . . ."[36] The Mozart "Requiem" ends and brings
him back to the present, but he shifts quickly into the past
again and again, in pendulum sweeps back and forth from the
album to the past to seek his identity. In the first chapter his
ancestral home is the geographical point of departure, to France,
to his university days, to Sergio, his sexual initiation, the 1956
revolt, his course in political economy given by Professor Ayuso
in 1951, to forty-eight hours previously with the announcement
of Ayuso's death. The second chapter uses the funeral of two
days before as the departure point. Since the entire novel is
a journey in time, one sample of his temporal jump will suffice.
During his first university year he visited Sergio who presented
him to his mother. She tells him: "Call me Ana and use the
familiar you . . . If not, we shall never be friends." Without any
transition at all, or even spacing, he is again close to the present,
in 1963. "Some days previous (it was sunny, the children were
feeding the pigeons, the urban guard was passing by with his
showy uniform and the entire city offered to the unwary a
radiant aspect of happiness) you had parked your car on the
shining avenue of the Cathedral like one of the millions of
tourists who for some weeks past. . . ." After looking at the
apartment where Sergio and his mother had lived, now apparently closed, he wonders what might have happened to Ana.
Again without transition, we are back in 1951. "Sergio has talked
to me so much about you that in reality it is as though we
already know one another."[37]

As in his other novels, we encounter strange types, "a bald-
headed syphilitic resembling Frankenstein and singing boleros,"
along with lyrical descriptions which occur throughout the novel.
"Night had fallen without your noticing it, and, seated still in
the garden, you could not distinguish the versatile flight of the
swallows nor the reddish fringe of twilight on the sinuous profile
of the mountains."[38] "As the land became elevated you could

distinguish the tombs situated at the foot of the hill, escorted by the dark green of the cypress and, at a distance, the angry blue sea, the crane and the light house of the jetty, the boats anchored at the mouth of the port . . . The wearied summer sun seemed to delay in setting, but the violence of the wind presaged a shower. Over the fortress of Montjuich sporadic clouds, advance guard of a threatening and sombre army, occupied strategic positions in an evasive sky, transparent, colorless. . . ."[39]

As in previous novels he employs his repetitive devices in a kind of "veni, vidi, vici" technique. "They were beginning to speak scornfully of the venality, grossness and petit bourgeois spirit of the French."[40] ". . . awaiting the instant—weeks, months or years later—to arch his eyebrows, or pick his gums with a toothpick or display his newspaper ostentatiously in the midst of the violent and feverish discourse. . ."[41]

The novel is more psychologically oriented than previous ones, and intensifies elements such as flashback, political analysis, and interior monologue, present in his other works. The extreme involvement with form as well as the philosophical introspection into the meaning of what it is to be a man, faced with the inevitable prospect of a final end, is new. In its neo-realistic existential and temporal and mythic projections, *Signs of Identity* may well deserve the accolade afforded it by José Agustín, one of the fine young Mexican novelists, who calls it "the most important Spanish novel of the century."[42]

V The Mature Novels (Conclusion)

Goytisolo's "mature" novels, to use his own assessment, simply intensify the elements already present in his work almost from the first moment: his lack of grammatical nicety, his faithful transcription of Spanish society (faithful in spite of an occasional almost grotesque evaluation of characters and their motivations, the absurd appellations in *La resaca*, the exaggerated portrayal of super-sexual athletes in *La isla*, the depersonalization of characters in *Fin de fiesta*), his photographic eye, his pessimistic view of society, the omnipresent Catholic Church (less emphatically present in *Señas de identidad*), his use of flashbacks, interior monologue, and temporal experimentation. The more detailed documentation and pseudo-objectivism does not defeat Goytisolo's identification with his characters (indeed, in the case of Alvaro Mendiola, Goytisolo is the character, suffering the same strongly felt subconscious and intensely personal projection of his childhood, adolescence, and maturity). The grimness, his improved exterior vision, the deforming neo-realism, the reportorial objectivity, fails to destroy the emotional vigor and sense of immediate and inner experience. The total effect of these works conveys an impression, not only of man's inhumanity to man, but of a world where at times the normal passions and sympathies, qualities of being human, are either frustrated or so exaggerated that they cease reflecting true humanity. Giner, Antonio, Claudia, Dolores, and Alvaro, the most persuasive characterizations, cannot disguise the triviality, pettiness, inhumanity, and general hopelessness of their society, a picture so bleak that it overshadows the characters as people to convert them into representatives of certain segments of the Spanish world, a cruel and destructive place which has no room for humanity. With the possible exception of Alvaro, the characters can live intensely for a moment but are not sufficiently "created" to maintain their individuality throughout the novel. Nevertheless, in spite of Goytisolo's stated rejection on several occasions of the psychological novel, Dolores, Giner, and Alvaro are psychologically well developed, even if they lack the fascinating abnormalities of the more poetic creations of his earlier works such as Estanislaa, Utah, and Uribe. Alvaro, especially, Goytisolo's major character creation, is a psychologically convincing twentieth-century man, a victim of his anguish, insufficiencies, insecurities, and hopelessness.

Goytisolo himself views the novel, whose actual chronological time of three days is infinitely expanded to carry its burden of Spanish resentment and disillusion, as a break with all his previous work. Completing the process he started with *La resaca*, he concentrates not so much on the Spain of the Civil War that was but the reality of the Spain that is and may be. Unlike previous novels which he based on a literary tradition only partly assimilated and digested by him, *Señas de identidad* includes, in its mixture of the colloquial and elegant, fragmentary elements deliberately not fully integrated into the novel so as to convey a geographical and temporal destruction. Goytisolo uses newspaper accounts, documents and pure invention to construct an almost skeleton-like structure which, he believes, helped implement both his stylistic and moral preoccupations. In his historical and socio-logical story of Spain and the contemporary scene he creates a burlesque version of the official government and describes the paradoxical quality of a regime dedicated to tradition and op-posed to progress which nonetheless welcomed the industrial revolution and destroyed thereby Spain's enchantment without obtaining the concomitant liberties experienced in more advanced countries.[43]

In his mature novels Goytisolo is concerned with human beings who face the knowledge of their certain death, realizing at the same time they must maintain the power of decision as to future acts. He sees man from a new perspective and projects his reality through at times strange symbols and structures which appeal to the multilevel perceptions of the reader. He employs a multiplicity of planes and superimposed structural levels, but he attempts, at the same time, to avoid novelistic exaggeration which would abort the impact on the reader. Although from time to time he has flirted with objectivist insistence on reality as perceived as the present, he has not allowed structure and style to overshadow plot nor has he indulged in an overaccumulation of details of things observed. Goytisolo gives artistic form to and extracts the esthetic possibilities from ordinary life. In his search for authentic values in a society without them and in the expression of his own reality, he has achieved a form which involves esthetic experience in its relationship to his ethics and his protagonists' role in a modern and often absurd world.

Goytisolo is, in the final analysis, concerned with human and social values. His characters, both the oppressors and the victims, may be capable of salvation, and thus Goytisolo ex-amines, at times even provokes, certain states of conscience which may lead to a purifying political action, not divorced from artistic values. Although his latest novel provides a pessi-mistic picture of a closed situation without apparent hope, *Signs of Identity*, his clearest political statement, in portraying the political history of twentieth-century Spain, may serve a clarifying if not cathartic purpose. It may be that when the reader has forgotten the purely artistic experimentation, he will remember the sorrows of the Spanish people.

When one reads critical material about Goytisolo, the two words which seem to occur with relative frequency are objectivism and neorealism. The former, with its movie techniques that describe both people and objects externally without personal interpretation, as we have seen, has not been fully followed by Goytisolo. In his novels he has abstained from comments at times but not from direct intervention and psychological penetration, of a sort, into his characters, forbidden to a true objectivist. His latest novel clearly has little connection with objectivism. As for the neorealism, Goytisolo attacks, albeit not always so directly as the truly dedicated social realist, the status quo, and wants to change the social, political, and moral environment of Spain. While Goytisolo has never belonged to either the objectivists or the social realists with complete dedication, he has used their techniques, along with many others, but he has always been too keenly aware of the literary movements of Europe and America and the infinite possibilities of artistic creation to function absolutely within the esthetic limitations imposed by any movement.

Short Stories, Travel Fiction
and Literary Criticism

I To Live Here (*Para vivir aquí*), 1960

PARA VIVIR AQUÍ is a collection of short stories written for the most part during 1957 and 1958. Very little happens in the stories, as the author characteristically depends on settings and the evocation of people and places through an accumulation of details and a slowing of time. A series of incidents, often unrelated to the theme, presents us with prostitutes, soldiers, lovers, students, and tourists. Many of Goytisolo's short stories, for example, *El encierro* (The Confinement),[1] have been published in reviews, and others, such as "Cara y Cruz," the first story in *Para vivir aquí*, have been translated into English.[2]

"Cara y Cruz" ("Face and Cross") again presents us with the Eucharist Congress which is coming to town. It makes its presence felt in all places, and its shields go up on all the houses, including that of the local house of prostitution. To keep the town pure for the Nuncio who is arriving, the authorities decide to transfer all the prostitutes to the countryside and outlying towns. A young man and his friend decide to go after them. The girls are exhausted and more than willing to exchange their favors for a decent place to sleep. One of the boys, Borés, offers one of the prostitutes his father's office. The men and girls spend their time drinking. One of the men says: "We should have congresses like this every year . . . don't you think so?" The narrator answers him: "I answered him that he was right, and, if my memory serves me right, I believe we had a drink together."[3]

In "Suburbios" ("Suburbs") Alvarito looks up his student friend with whom he often got drunk and sought out excitement. Alvarito tells his friend that he has had a quarrel with his father

and has been told to leave home. His father wants him to marry
Memé, but he has gotten Laura, a lower-class girl, pregnant.
Meanwhile he arranges for a date with the daughter of a tavern
owner whom he meets after taking Laura to the movies and dining
with Memé. The story is filled with talk of women, dirty ones,
clean ones, women without teeth, and women with large breasts.
It has no real point except to give Goytisolo a chance for some
realistic dialogue between two rather disagreeable adolescents
about sex and women.

"Otoño, en el puerto, cuando llovizna" ("Autumn in the Port
When it Drizzles") treats of a variety of types such as bored
students, fishermen, sellers of mussels, divers, dock workers, and
contrabandists, the raw material and humans that Goytisolo
knows best, and whom he describes with affection. They play
cards, drink, talk, and exhibit the camaraderie between men
which Goytisolo injects into most of his stories and novels. The
young law student learns from Raimundo, a friend whom he met
at the Varadero cafe and bar, about boats and various kinds of
fishing. His relationship to him resembles that of Pipo to the
Gorilla in *Fiestas*. The student goes off to Paris. As he looks
back on his past, as a boy of good family, a student and artist,
he realizes that basically the only authentic meaning in his life
was the Varadero and Raimundo, the landscape of fog in the
autumn when it used to drizzle and the waves were still.

"El viaje" ("The Voyage") continues the static representations
of life where almost nothing takes place. A couple comes to a
village for a vacation. They visit the beach, observe a broken
down circus which has been stranded in the town because it has
no money. They eat the insipid food at the inn, hire a boat for
a ride, and drive their car. The village had been well off at one
time, with a factory and a mining industry, but the industry had
given out, and the villagers had traveled to France, to Barcelona, and to America to find work. Those who remained spent
half the time in idleness, for in spite of the promises of the
Madrid authority, nothing was done to remedy their poverty-
stricken situation. The villagers, as one of them explains, could
only lower their heads and bite their fists from hunger.

The couple, bored with their sedentary life in Barcelona,
contemplate buying a house in the village as an ideal refuge.

The young son of the hotel owner polishes their car, and on their drive they see factory ruins, a band of crows, the dry land, poor and scraggly vegetation, and finally the beach. They sun themselves and bathe. Deciding that the country life is as brutalizing as that of the city, they travel, only to find the same bad roads, bad food, and boredom. They come across the circus again and learn to their surprise that it has been successful. On their return to the inn they discover that the town council, in order to enable the circus to pay off its debts, had authorized it—and its six girls—to serve as a brothel to the three hundred townspeople. The priest had protested somewhat but finally had washed his hands of the affair, some thought because he had been bought off. He later celebrated a solemn mass for the pardon of sins.

"La Guardia" ("The Guard") concerns a sergeant who is transferred to a prison compound of dangerous soldiers, illiterate criminal types for the most part. Among them is one who borrowed and lost money not belonging to him to bet on a "sure" thing in the football pool since he can never fulfill his dreams of being a football star.

In "La Ronda" ("The Night Patrol") a couple visits Cartagena where they stroll, eat, and observe life around them. They encounter a soldier patrol stationed in the town. Gonzalo López Rosas, known to all as Macanas, the best dancer in the city, agrees to dance for them. The soldiers take advantage of him (forcing him to dance for their entertainment) because there is so little to do in the town. The couple recall the incident eleven months later.

"Los Amigos" ("The Friends") deals with a version of a protest march called by university students and others. The friends go to a bar which a police inspector had fined because he claimed it was full of prostitutes. In the conversation the boys attack the national press, the government, and the army. " 'It is one of our glorious soldiers,' I said. 'Of our glorious Saviours,' corrected Julia. . . . 'We are in a free country,' protested Antony. 'In an organic democracy,' said Julia."[4] One of the customers, a soldier wounded by the Loyalists, sings the National Hymn, and the others accompany him in a parody. The bouncers throw him out into the street. The owner feels no affection or

gratitude for those who have fought a war and thus give themselves an air of importance.

Goytisolo dedicated "Aquí Abajo" ("Here Below"), the final
and longest story in the volume, to his brother Luis. As with almost all his stories, very little happens, and he makes constant
use of description to slow time, as well as references to time
segments to create a feeling of "déjà vu." "The sky was clouding
over for a storm, and the sea was discolored and grey in its
agitation. The waves overlapped like the scales on the back of
a gigantic fish. From time to time, one stood out for a few
seconds, like a wing. I recall that the shore was covered with
algae and dozens of sea gulls flew around me, with their wings
unfolded, in the form of a fan."[5]

Emiliano, with whom the narrator—all the stories are told in
the first person—had played as a boy, studied at the university,
wandered through the streets, and visited whore houses, has
changed a great deal when the narrator returns from a two-
year stay in France, paid for by his father. Emiliano and his
university group have taken up activities against the régime,
and he asks his friend to join. The latter, restless and without
any real roots, decides instead to fulfill his military service obli-
gation of six months. Still restless, he wanders the streets and
takes up with a whore. He engages in conversations about the
previous war and the sufferings endured by the Blue Division.
He enters into a relationship with Herminia, whose husband is
a traveling salesman.

He learns that in Madrid the students have called a strike.
The priest preaches the dangers to be found in the city, especially of the damage intellectuals can do to the poor soldiers
and prisoners. As one of the latter exclaims, however, " 'I should
like to know what that character calls dangers . . . I'm sure he
has never been hungry . . . And you? Have you been?' Gonzalo
turned his glance toward the ground. 'We poor people suffer
hunger our whole life . . . It is almost a sickness. We do not
know what it is to be full.' "[6] The narrator indulges in other
drunken brawls and whore-house adventures, and finally receives a letter which informs him that Emiliano has been taken
prisoner. He feels ashamed that while Emiliano and others have

been fighting for their ideals, he has been sleeping with a married woman he doesn't love, visiting bordellos and becoming drunk with his fellow officers. In the hope of accomplishing some positive action, he tries to teach the illiterate soldiers how to read. On his leave of absence he heads for home, thinking that it is not too late to indulge in the social action he had refused to face three months before.

These eight stories have definite anti-Franco overtones, as Goytisolo examines various facets of the Spanish myth about human liberty and peace and plenty for all. His female characters are generally somewhat pretty and stupid, but the boys, anxious to fill their empty lives with feverish activities, are fully aware of the Spanish tragedy.[7] The characters convey individual aspects of a collective frustration and despair endured by disaffected Spanish victims of tyranny.

The usual Goytisolo photographic realism is present. "I saw that the boy was unfastening his fly and, without paying any attention to the protests of the other, he urinated with a cruel satisfaction, into the ant hole."[8] The political and sociological implications can also be found, as one of the characters insists that Spaniards know only one language, that of the cudgel. When one beats and abuses them, they admire the abuser, and they need to be governed with a heavy hand and a big stick. On the other side of the coin one finds the idealism of Emiliano and his friends, the need for communication, love, and understanding, all components in Goytisolo's works.

In summarizing the technique Goytisolo uses, one may say that it resembles greatly that of Azorín in treating as poetry the vulgar and even trivial daily occurrences. Literature and life become indistinguishable, and it is a credit to Goytisolo's artistic temperament that he can reproduce the monotony of human existence without completely boring the reader. Short stories, by their very structure, usually open on a brief and intensely experienced moment of time. Goytisolo allows himself the luxury of a long temporal development and exploration, the technique of the novel, and rarely offers an intense and momentary dramatic experience, so common to the short story.

II *Travel Literature*

With *La resaca*, Goytisolo began to travel around the city
of Barcelona to discover the relationships existing between
man and his environment, and to examine man as a reflection
of his existence. Taking a leaf from the new narrative genre
which Camilo José Cela had started with *Viaje a la Alcarria*
(Voyage to the Alcarria) and continued through three other travel
volumes, and feeling his responsibility as a writer, Goytisolo studied for four years before writing his first report on an odyssey,
Campos de Níjar (Fields of Níjar), 1960. He felt that travel literature required a long investigation, research, and documentation, for it combined the social, the historical, and the lyric. His
description of cities and countryside not only reflects Cela's
technique but also vaguely recalls descriptions in the works
of the authors of the Generation of '98, although his motives
and methods are apparently distinctive. In *Juegos de manos*
one can find most of the elements of the thoughts and construction developed throughout his later novels, and his narrative,
La Chanca, to be discussed below, shows a style which ger-
minated almost a decade earlier. The imagery, the settings, the
texture of his travel or fictionalized personal narrative themselves may be found, not only in *La resaca,* but in most of his
earlier novels as well.

Campos de Níjar describes his trip to an impoverished area
of Spain in southeastern Andalusia where the people live under
primitive and almost hopelessly desolate conditions. In his work,
which the author labels simply "narratives," The narrator talks
with the underprivileged, with city workers, and with poor farm-
ers. He visits villages where people start to work when they are
children, where they suffer and die. As one of the characters says:
"They say that the world is changing and that soon we shall reach
the moon, but for us all the days are the same."[9] He writes in
the first person, as a kind of witness, a technique he started
with *La isla (The Island)*, and presents deeds as they occur.
They are saved from a guide book recital by his talent and
his poetic pen. He recalls his first view of Almería. "I remember very well the profound impression of violence and poverty

which Almería produced on me, as I traveled along national Highway 340, the first time that I visited it some years ago."[10] He alternates continuous descriptions of the landscape of this traditional section of Spain with conversations and dialogues of the people, which reveal their joys and sorrows, their dignity and hunger. The individuals who inhabit his documentary are alive and aware in the present; shots of life in process, even if some of the interpersonal relationships found in more orthodox novels are not apparent, create the impression of fiction. "As the sun approaches the crest of the mountains, the countryside takes on a golden color. The truck descends and climbs and from time to time shows for a moment on level ground. We crossed another rocky stream bed. The vegetation is scanty, dwarf fig trees, brambles and an agave or so. Above us the sky remains blue, unchanging."[11]

The first impression—wild and inhospitable—which Níjar inspires in the traveler who comes along the road of Los Pipaces, disappears with proximity. The outskirts of the town are rough, but the effort of man has transformed the countryside harmoniously. The mountain slope is tiered with built up terraces. Fruit trees and almond trees alternate on the yellowish steep cliffs and the olive trees hang over the steepest part of the incline like some run-away flocks . . . "Today is market day," says one of my companions. "All those people you see are from the farms." "What do they sell?" "Whatever they have. Pigs, chickens, eggs . . . With what they get they buy bread and oil for the rest of the week. They are people who live in isolated spots, several miles from one another, and they only come to town on Saturdays."
Along the street there came women dressed in black and a gypsy seated astride a donkey. The house of Níjar are of a single floor and have whitewashed façades but, different from those of El Barranquete or Los Nietos, their aspect is somewhat African and recall rather that of the dwellings of the towns in upper Andalusia and Extremadura.[12]

Goytisolo takes time out from his "narrations" to comment on an ironical statement Ortega y Gasset once made about the future belonging to "admirable Níjar." He accuses Ortega of fickleness and misplaced irony in his attack on the inhabitants of Níjar who have a long history and tradition. It was not the people who wasted money but rather the select minorities of which Ortega spoke. Goytisolo feels the minorities are guilty and the people are their victims. Ironically, Goytisolo proves Ortega's idea that the novel lends itself

more easily than any other literary form to absorbing elements alien to art. Within the novel almost anything fits: science, religion, sociology, esthetic criticism—if only it is ultimately derealized and confined within the inner world of the novel; i.e., if it remains without actual and effective validity. In other words, a novel can contain as much sociology as it desires but the novel itself cannot be sociological. The dose of alien elements a book can bear . . . depends on the author's capability of dissolving them in the atmosphere of the novel as such . . . Not in the invention of plots but in the invention of interesting characters lies the best hope of the novel.[13]

By combining description and conversations with the inhabitants in their refreshing dialect about their lives and experiences, and by correlating these with his own, Goytisolo has created a work which fits Ortega's definition, as well as that of Camilo José Cela, which we shall examine later in this chapter. Goytisolo describes the unfortunate physical condition of the inhabitants, living in a climate where years and years have passed without any rain:

". . . and my wife and I sowing barley stupidly, hoping for some miracle . . . One summer everything dried up and we had to sacrifice the animals. A donkey that I bought when the war ended, too. You can't imagine what it was like . . ."
The plain smokes about us. A flock of crows flies cawing toward Níjar. The sky continues imperturbably blue. The song of the cicadas springs forth like a deaf protest from the soil. "We only live on prickly pears. The land doesn't serve for anything else. When we suffered hunger we filled our stomach to the bursting point."[14]

Often, not content with the description and the dialogue, the author interjects his own experience. In this connection it is difficult to accept one critic's idea that "the countryside is only a pretext for public confession and an occasion for exhibitionism."[15] Goytisolo uses words as instruments to convey his own emotions and experience, but he uses a personal interjection as one further means of narrative deceleration in order to fill each temporal segment and help focus attention on the two important elements, man and nature, in their interdependence.

I remember Garrucha, with its factories and foundries in ruins, and I think that the mining crisis of Almería must have been a fairly generalized phenomenon. In all the homes in the provinces one remembers it as a true calamity . . . Of the numerous explanations which I have heard about its origin and possible causes—indifference of the governments, inadaptability to modern methods, Catalan industrial competition—none has satisfied me completely, and, hoping that someone better prepared than I complete the findings some day, I invite scholars to go through the old mining centers of the province, with their houses in ruins, their squares deserted and their driftways and wells flooded.[16]

Goytisolo is not the narrator who analyzes the spiritual crisis of Spain, but he is an actor in the drama he depicts and a member of the set he is describing.

Goytisolo concludes that if one is to be poor, as people in Níjar are, it is well to want to be ugly, also. "I wanted to tell them that, if we were poor, the best that we might desire was to be ugly also; for beauty would serve us as a pretext to cross our arms and in order to come out from within ourselves we ought to resist the temptation to feel ourselves a picture postcard or museum piece.

"That's why Almería pleases me. Because it has no Giralda nor an Alhambra. Because it does not try to cover itself with clothes and ornaments. Because it is a naked, true land. . ."[17]

Before discussing *La Chanca*, let us examine Camilo José Cela's travel literature. He has written five of these excursions into the soul of Spain: *Viaje a la Alcarria* (*Trip to Alcarria*), 1948; *Del Miño al Bidasoa* (*From the Miño to the Bidasoa*), 1952; *Judíos moros y cristianos* (*Jews, Moors and Christians*), 1956; *Primer viaje andaluz* (*First Andalusian Voyage*), 1959; and *Viaje al Pirineo de Lérida* (*Trip to the Pyrenee of Lérida*), 1964. While Cela has never insisted that these works are novels, he mentions that Gallimard, in the French edition of *Viaje a la Alcarria*, calls it a novel. He claims the reason he himself did not do so "was in order not to complicate things more than they are."[18]

It is interesting in this connection to realize that Cela has advocated for some time a new concept of the novel. In the prologue to the second edition of *Mrs. Caldwell habla con su hijo,* he says:

I have collected definitions of the novel, I have read everything on this subject which has fallen into my hands, I have written some articles, I have given various lectures and I have thought constantly and with all the rigor of which I may be capable on the theme and, finally, I find that I do not know, nor do I believe that anybody knows, what, in truth, a novel is. It is possible that the only sensible definition which might be given of this genre is that of saying that "novel" is everything which, edited in the form of a book, admits under the title, and parenthetically, the word "novel."[19]

Cela has shown himself to be a critic of the traditional forms of the novel and against those he feels are self-appointed guardians of the status quo. He wishes these critics would invent a new genre and stop trying to kill literature in order to be able to examine the quiet corpse at leisure.[20] He believes, along with Baroja and Goytisolo, that life is what lives within us or without us, and that the author serves as its conveyance. He disclaims any boundaries at all to the genre of the novel and feels that all attempts to limit or define it are idle.

As late as 1965 Cela explained that he still believed in his definition of the open novel. "The novel, what we call novel in a tacit manner and without being too much in agreement with what we want to say, is like a child who has grown without order . . . was born with Adam and Eve . . . or it has not yet been born . . . A novelist is one who writes novels; what is denied to us is what is the novel, that is, that which the novelist writes. Some day with computers or with great patience and thousands of years all novels might be written. Then one might have, perhaps a vague conclusion as to what a novel is."[21]

Camilo José Cela has written some of his best stylistic prose about his many travels through Spain. His picturesque descriptions and authentic atmosphere he reproduces (what he sees and communicates) are as novelistic as any of his novels, even though his purpose is to communicate to others the immediacy he feels in his experience. He agrees with Pío Baroja that the novel requires a skeleton on which to drape its flesh, but he conceives of the skeleton of the novel as a series of vertebrae or loose episodes which may be linked in a new way. In his travel books, or narratives, he describes the psychology of his characters, the real and the fictitious, in a fictional manner which the objective novel with its photographic attention to detail and its elimination of psychological implications cannot equal. Cela's travel novels reflect modern tension, document human pain, sorrow, and ugliness, and convey the soul of the people of Castile, Andalusia, Galicia, and other sections of Spain. He wishes to assault the reader's nostrils with the smells of Spain, his ears with its sounds, his eyes with its colors, his soul with its sorrows. The real types he presents are fictional also in the best sense of the word, and he includes a fictional episode from time to time, as well as lyrical evocations of a real geography.

If Cela's contention is valid, and the distinctions between the genres are becoming more difficult to maintain, can we accept fully Ortega's statement as to the importance of character creation in the novel? Goytisolo has only incidentally created characters, and few are multi-faceted. Yet some of the people who appear in *Campos de Níjar* have more literary life than many of the characters found in composite novels such as Cela's *La colmena* (*The Hive*). A variety of post-Civil War works such as *Plaza del Castillo* by Rafael García Serrano combine personal narrative with a light novelesque thread and may well be listed as contemporary chronicles. Goytisolo's work, however, peopled by real people enmeshed each in his own circumstances, gives the appearance of fiction as he probes deeply at a segment of Spanish life whose essence he seeks to capture. In his work, ultimately about people, Goytisolo becomes more than a mere recorder, serving as an actor in the work, and the real situations assume the appearance of a fictionalized account. If *Campos de Níjar* and the documentaries which follow it are not novels in the classic sense, neither are they travel books only. While his "documentaries" contain some objective, almost photographic reproductions of the reality he is conveying, they also convert that reality, in all its desolation and dullness, into a novelistic and lyrical experience, in which he includes himself as narrator and participant, and thus he creates in the reader's mind the feeling that he is reading a novel. *Campos de Níjar* is one aspect of Goytisolo's proposal, shared with Cela as already mentioned, that literature is life. Not everybody is willing to accept the fictional quality of this work. For one critic, *"Campos de Níjar* and *La Chanca* are not novels. The author calls them narrations. Let us call them explorations."[22] Yet, according to two other well known writers: "If one learns anything about fiction from reading even a limited number of short stories and novels, it is that there is no single special technique or formula for writing good fiction. Rather one learns that every good writer develops a method which, in so far as he is a good writer, is specially adapted to the kind of effect which he is trying to give."[23]

La Chanca, 1962

Another documentary or travel novel, *La Chanca* paints a continuing picture of misery and poverty in the arid region of Almería in Andalusia and of the fishing district, known as La Chanca, within that region. Goytisolo, somewhat fictionalized and younger, recalls his youth and the dilemma of the Spaniard who lives outside of Spain. He had left Spain to breathe the cultural freedom of Europe, but after the first period of excitement and new discovery, he suffered the same loss of orientation and felt the same nostalgia that all Spaniards outside of their country feel, a nostalgia swept away only through a reidentification, preferably through physical presence, with the Spanish *pueblo*. "They were years of waiting, of impatient search, during which I had lived as if in the air. And, suddenly, when I was almost in despair, I again heard the familiar music and the music was confused with the voice of my people, forming with it a single entity and returning to me intact my lost youth and the warmth of thirty million brothers."[24]

While in France he encounters Vitorino, an exile from Almería, who was one of those who took up his gun and fought so that injustice might end. But twenty years had passed, and now he no longer talked. Vitorino tells him that he has a young cousin, called the Cartagenero, Antonio Roa, who lives in La Chanca. Goytisolo promises to look him up. When he visits

Antonio's home he discovers that the police had taken him away ten days earlier. Through Antonio's family and friends, Goytisolo meets many people and learns about Almería, La Chanca, and by implication, Spain. As in his other works, the people protest that they do not have enough to eat, and to support their families many go to France to earn a living. Goytisolo describes the fair, the marketplace, the poorly dressed men, the blind lottery-ticket sellers, and the Almerían prostitutes. As he travels through La Chanca, he sees garbage, flies, leprosy, trachoma, cancer, and madness in the inhabitants. He finds hungry children to whom food means more than toys, people who must steal to live, and priests who are unconcerned with the problems of the poor.

Goytisolo reflects that La Chanca "is a universe apart in which the visitor feels like a foreigner . . . and the groups of women, old men and children who root and maraud in the rubbish? Dressed, shod, protected from the onslaught of the sun with smoked glasses, what kind of bond exists between him and them?

"I asked myself these and other questions and, no matter how much I racked my brain, I couldn't find the answer. The uneasiness I felt resisted all reason. It was a mixture of restlessness and anxiety—like the feeling of being excess baggage there. . ."[25]

When he meets Roa's family, he learns that La Chanca lacks doctors, a dispensary, nurses, a market, and, in the majority of the houses, electricity. The inhabitants have to carry water, at times from hundreds of yards away. The grandmother tells him of their sufferings, of how her husband, an honorable man, was driven to steal in order to feed his family, and she finally asks him: "You who have studied and traveled a great deal, tell me: to be good and honorable, isn't that enough?"[26]

Goytisolo concludes that in La Chanca and in Spain that is not enough. Overwhelmed by what he has seen and experienced, his blood boils; he feels anguished, useless, and as though it were a knife in his side, he remembers the geography book he had used in school which stated that Almería was a Spanish province. "Almería is not a Spanish province. Almería is a Spanish possession occupied militarily by the Civil Guard. Century after century, the indifference of successive governments has ruined its resources and reduced it to its actual condition as a colony. The citizen of Almería, enslaved in his district, emigrates and is exploited even in the industrial regions of Spain. Economic discrimination pursues him wherever he looks for a living."[27]

Goytisolo becomes drunk, and in his stupor dreams of his experiences and that he is talking to Vitorino about La Chanca, a land without sun, without air, without trees. When he awakens, dawn is breaking, and the "daily sun is beginning to tinge the sky of La Chanca."[28]

La Chanca contains a series of appendices which describe Almería at various stages of its history from the twelfth century on. They contain figures on the number of caves and shacks, the complete lack of doctors, watchmen, fountains, post offices, and electricity for most of the 19,000 inhabitants of the district. One concludes, after reading *La Chanca*, along with José María Pérez Lozano, a writer who visited La Chanca and wrote about it: "One hears this word and his stomach heaves. La Chanca, My God!"[29]

Goytisolo's first-person narrative in which he is an actor presents us with deeds examined from an immutable point of view. The reader must accept the author's judgment and has no fixed value which stems from the narration itself to enable him to form an objective opinion. Goytisolo as author, realizing that the reader may distrust the narrator as actor, presents the documents to bolster his findings and reduce the alternate possibilities a reader might imagine. Descriptions by a narrator-author will represent the author's feelings and interpretation of the facts as he sees them. The reader, further removed, sees almost as a mirror image what the narrator allows him to see. At times Goytisolo speaks to us of his feelings and experiences; at others he includes the conversations of the characters around him, which serves to put them and the author on the same plane of reality. Goytisolo's search for Roa's family helps unite his literary framework with the vision of society he wishes to document.

Goytisolo again becomes a part of his literature in his sympathetic, direct, and detailed account of the agony of a people living in physical degradation in which they are sustained only by a vague dignity. His infusion of feeling into a natural backdrop is intended to intensify one's reactions to the misery he displays. The grandmother, Luiso, and the others, in reaction to their suffering, reveal their souls, as does La Chanca, and if his work is not fiction, in its artistry, it creates the effect of fiction. It might be argued that Goytisolo offers here, not only the deplorable conditions found in a certain type of society, but also deeply held convictions about man's nature. His work is tied to time, for as the history of Spain is being written, his work is being written, and both the author and his work occupy a role in the society he views. He is conditioned by his reality and the time in which he lives, and his work, in a state of flux, is not yet complete. Goytisolo recognizes that decisive changes may occur in Spain in the 1960's which may eventually date his sociological documentation but will destroy neither the historicity nor the humanity of what he has written.

Pueblo en marcha (*People on the March*), 1963

Goytisolo called this work "snapshots of a trip to Cuba" where he spent two and one half months traveling, living and eating with the *pueblo,* whom he found "dignified and noble." *Pueblo en marcha* contains the same mixture of countryside, dialogue, and social reality found in *Campos de Níjar* and in *La Chanca,* but it presents reality in a less fictionalized manner and is more of a travelogue.

Goytisolo recalls his youth as a member of the privileged classes of society, and his family's relationship to Cuba through their sugar mills there. The Second World War opened his eyes regarding the menace of socialism, as viewed by his elders, and he thought of taking refuge in Cuba. When he studied law at the university, he first began to have a social conscience, especially with regard to the responsibility of his own family for the misery of Cubans. Discovering some painful letters from his grandfather's slaves, he became aware of his false values and bourgeois respectability, and Cuba became a personal reproach. In 1958, impressed by the possibility of incorporating an idea into reality, his doubts disappeared as the incipient revolution confirmed his new awareness of life, and he realized that to defend Cuba was to defend Spain, as twenty-five years earlier, to die in Spain was to die for Cuba.

When Goytisolo came to Manzanillo, which reminded him of Andalusia, much as Havana recalled Málaga, it seemed that he had known the city all his life. The signs stating that the houses were Cuban and that Cubans were prepared to defend them and their Fatherland to the death impressed him. He met the peasants, listened to political orators, and came to realize that their communism meant for them the betterment of the lot of the poor. The peasants were warm and generous. One who had lived in ignorance under Batista believed his boss was good because he gave him Christmas gifts, not realizing that he was being robbed injustly.

The usual peasant dialogues and direct descriptions of the people and places he saw are interspersed with lyrical pictures of sea gulls flying around floating palisades and the reflection of the light on the water. "As the sun warms up, the clouds dissolve and disappear. Some miles farther on the sky is intensely blue. The keys perturb the regularity of the horizon like deceitful mirages. The wind has completely subsided and the wake of the keel opens a furrow of foam on the quiet face of the water."[30] He learns the history of Cuba under Batista from the people's point of view, their lack of schooling, medicine, housing; their high infant mortality rate; the police terror and torture. Now "men asleep for centuries have awakened suddenly to their possibility as authentic men. A new sentiment goes through the island from one section to another. In Manzanillo it transforms and beautifies the face of men and women, old and young. One's heart warms and beats with joy on recognizing it: it is called fraternity."[31]

Goytisolo continues to intervene as a participant in the action to give us his impression of a new world being born, the improvement in education for children and adults, the clothing and food they never before enjoyed. Children who before did not eat meat or bread, did not read or write, gather without fear around Goytisolo. The peasant still works hard, but now he feels it is for his family and children, and he clears ground and builds houses and schools eagerly. Especially impressive for Goytisolo is the campaign against illiteracy eagerly undertaken by many city people who live separated from their families; rising with the sun and working all day, they carry instruction to hundreds of thousands of people.

He goes on a fishing trip and drinks beer with the soldiers and fisherfolk. The latter, originally tyrannized by the government which jailed or shot a man at the slightest provocation, now have their dignity as human beings. Goytisolo is impressed by the moral transformation of Cubans who have finally realized their authenticity as human beings. His informants tell him that while not all prejudice has disappeared, things are better. They hate the United States and would rather die than return to their former life.

Goytisolo shows us family scenes of a father hugging his child and simple men doing their jobs; he reveals their naïve and almost superstitious faith in Fidel Castro, whom they view as their Saviour. Goytisolo identifies with his friends Juan Angel, Manuel, Ramón's friends, the fisherfolks, and the school teacher. Undoubtedly *Pueblo en marcha* is Goytisolo's most propagandistic work, written with a fervor which overcame his esthetic judgment from time to time. Goytisolo has since tempered somewhat his judgments on the Cuban Revolution, but in 1962 he saw it as a defense of human dignity, not only for Cuba but for the entire world, as he concluded: "If they must die, let us die also with them."[32]

III *Goytisolo as Critic*

We have already seen Goytisolo's ideas about the novel as he expressed them in *Problemas de la novela* (*Problems of the Novel*) and in the polemic carried on with Guillermo de Torre in *Insula*. His interest in all phases of Spanish literature has continued, and he has written a number of articles for literary reviews.

In his articles written for *Cuadernos de Ruedo Ibérico*, a journal established in Paris in June, 1965, he shows special interest in the social values of literary manifestations. He attacks the Generation of Ninety-Eight, not only as ineffectual, but also as a sterile and paralyzing burden inherited by the new generation of writers who have problems which differ from those of their predecessors. The twenty-five years of dogmatism practiced by the Franco regime have contributed to the intellectual conformity, not only among liberals but even among Marxists, and the current essays produced in Spain, full of erudition and respect for gods and semi-gods of the past, show the least originality of any in the last two hundred years. During the dictatorship of Primo de Rivera, the values of Modernism and of the Generation of Ninety-Eight were criticized, but after the Spanish Civil War many of its members were considered voices of orthodoxy by the Fascists. As a result of the cultural break caused by the Spanish Civil War, a continuation of the culture represented by the figures of Ninety-Eight seemed necessary, even to non-Fascists, to provide a bridge to the future. But by 1955, the year Ortega died, the members of the "generation of the half century" already had their bridge. When the literary voices of their "Fathers" such as Sender, Aub, and Cernuda had been stilled and the authors persecuted, the ensuing orthodoxy furthered the greater importance of the literature of their grandfathers.

When Goytisolo and his generation criticized Ortega y Gasset as an assertion of their future liberty, they did not desire to do away with their literary inheritance, but rather to modify it in conformity with their new age. Their disrespect, if there was any, was much less than that the Generation of Ninety-Eight showed to writers, such as Galdós, of preceding generations. Nevertheless, Goytisolo and the fellow writers of his generation were accused of sacrilege, because the literary inheritance of the Generation of Ninety-Eight had become a cult, and instead of serving as a bridge to the future, had become a wall against it. Thus, ten years later, in 1965, when France, for example, had ceased basing its culture for some thirty years on the work of Bergson, Gide, or Valéry, Spanish criticism still operated around the writers of Ninety-Eight (Goytisolo is imprecise in his definition of the movement). Since the neocapitalistic Spain of 1965 differed from the world known by Unamuno and Ortega, their literary work could not serve in the current culture.

Deadened by twenty-five years of dictatorship, says Goytisolo, the critical spirit in Spain today is at its lowest ebb in all history, nor was fear of exercising freedom of judgment ever greater. Moreover, the cult of the Ninety-Eighters has succeeded in sterilizing contemporary essayists, and no real literary criticism is coming out of Spain. Even the Marxists, instead of trying to apply Marx's dialectical approach to the analysis of cultural and esthetic problems confronting Spain, mechanically copy formulas fifty years out of date. They write in 1965 as if the abolition of private property would automatically end the exploitation of man by man and wither away class prejudice. They too are victims, as are the cultists of Ninety-Eight, of a paralyzing inheritance and fear of heresy.

The remedy for the sad situation of Spanish criticism must come from the writers of his generation, themselves, who must be prepared to make their own errors, use their own criteria, and avoid the crutches of a doubtful respectability which might be theirs by aspiring to the officially exalted positions of the literary inquisitors and theologians.

Impressed by *Poesía y literatura* (*Poetry and Literature*), 1965, the posthumous publication of Luis Cernuda, a fine surrealistic poet in his own right, Goytisolo comments briefly on the types of literary criticism in France: university positivism; ideological, especially Marxist, best exemplified by Goldmann; existentialist, still based on Sartre's work; psychoanalytic, represented by Bachelard; structural, furthered by Levi-Strauss and Barthes; and finally formalist criticism, visibly headed by Robbe-Grillet and some of the practitioners of the so-called "new novel." In the twentieth century, thanks to new findings in anthropology, sociology, and psychoanalysis, literary criticism has undergone great changes, especially in the last thirty years. The danger is no longer from a traditional type, easily recognized for what it is, but from new criticism which, instead of using the variety of instruments available to it, limits itself to a single level, thus becoming totalitarian, monolithic, and dogmatic, prone to confuse the part for the whole. As samples he cites the attack of Sartre on Baudelaire, Lukacs against Proust, and the almost pathological insistence of Robbe-Grillet that he is the sole arbiter of the novel. When the latter, turning critic, attempts to condemn "engagé" literature, his efforts are as feeble as his method, based on an uncertain value system which is itself a product of the ideology of the moment. Cernuda, avoiding such restrictions, instead of condemning a work which does not meet a narrow formula, attempts to approach it from different points of view and with different techniques, adapting his criticism to the work instead of trying to force the work into a rigid mold. Cernuda inherits his flexible criteria not from the Spanish but rather from English and American critics.

In Spain, in spite of the thousands of articles and columns appearing under the name of criticism in books, newspapers, radio, and on television, the themes worked to death by the Generation of Ninety-Eight still prevail. Furthermore, quantity has not been matched by a corresponding quality. Goytisolo agrees with Cernuda that there is something foreign to literary criticism in the Spanish mentality, and although exceptions might be named, even they devoted themselves largely to erudition, glossing, and commenting, rather than to real criticism. Tradition is an unmoving force, and past authoritative opinion has become dogma. Culture cannot be exclusively inherited but must be fought for day by day and forged by each generation, with an independence of judgment impossible in Spain. Goytisolo reflects on the almost absurd preoccupation with medieval Spanish poetry, criticism valuable in its day but currently exaggerated beyond all reality. We might all learn a lesson, says Goytisolo, from reading Cernuda's work, so different from the official and officious saccharine criticism which seeks to equate the fatuous rhetoric of Rubén Darío, which has no meaning in the modern world, with the even more remote Bécquer, who nevertheless willed a new tradition to his descendants.

Goytisolo comments gratefully that his *Problems of the Novel* is out of print, for its contents were not carefully thought out. It is but one of many works such as Alfonso Sastre's *Anatomía del realismo* (*Anatomy of Realism*), 1965, sincerely presented but based on voluminous reading not fully digested. Above all, Spanish letters take themselves too seriously, using unmoving, unchanging critical values. What is needed in modern criticism is a sense of the humorous, but unfortunately, even this probably would not suffice, for intellectual liberty died long ago in Spain.

Goytisolo writes also on the development of scientific linguistics, the various theories on the origin and the meaning of language, the attitudes of writers and their responsibilities toward linguistic evolutionary process, the differences between written and spoken Spanish and its metamorphosis in Spanish America, the Negro influence on the Cuban language, and the necessity for flexibility in a living tongue.

His major collection of critical essays, *El furgón de cola* (The Caboose), appeared in 1967. In addition to the previously mentioned studies (all somewhat modified) from the *Cuadernos de Ruedo Ibérico,* this volume of thirteen essays includes articles on censorship, political and social problems, and Spanish writers. Goytisolo borrowed his title from an essay by Antonio Machado on Spanish culture, written in 1916: " 'We keep maintaining, faithful to our traditions, our position at the tail end of the caboose.' "[33]

Goytisolo, lamenting Spanish self-deprecation from 1800 on, contends that the concept of an "archaic Spain" no longer corresponds to reality. In spite of the apparent immobility of its political superstructure, Spain is experiencing profound structural alterations, and its acceptance of the modern industrial world implies further changes of a moral and cultural nature. The nobility, loyalty, and disinterestedness which supposedly characterized Spaniards until recent times have disappeared with the new industrial religion, "and with them disappear also, the sentimental and moral reasons for our adhesion to the cause of the *pueblo* which incarnated them."[34] The *pueblo,* which acted so bravely during the Spanish Civil War, because of its passivity in the post-Civil War years, must assume responsibility for its government. Goytisolo rejects the almost universally held concept that the Spaniard is a poor, sincere, passionate, and brave possessor of a "soul" which ordinary Europeans have misplaced. Europeans, in their esthetic admiration of "backward Spain," help support Spain's old structures which strive to petrify history.

Contact with tourists and work abroad have opened Spanish eyes to the possibility of a new monetary religion, but in copying the superficial aspects of foreign models without having had the social education and training so much a part of other nations, Spaniards have created a caricature, "showing us a society, and individual in the full process of formation, ambiguous and without character."[35] The myths of a pre-industrial nation offer only romantic escapism to the modern nonconformist intellectual whose choices seem limited to romantic rebellion or a role as a functionary without freedom of action. Intellectuals of Goytisolo's generation, now in their thirties, prepared for events which did not occur, and as a result, "the men of my generation find ourselves in the abnormal situation of growing old without having known either youth or responsibility."[36] Writers and intellectuals, unaware of the organic transformation of Spanish society, tilt at windmills in a universe populated by ghosts.

Spain is neither heroic nor noble. Immoral matrimonial and family relations, social hypocrisy, continual infidelity, and hidden envy have become chronic illnesses from which all Spaniards suffer. The mercantilization of human relations, an inferiority complex, idle imitation, self-satisfaction, and exploitation of so-called ancient virtues have created a country which, if it is not yet Europe, is, in any event, no longer Spain. Before Spain can recreate itself, it must be willing to face its reality, uncover the cowardice, hypocrisy, and egotism beneath its masks of pride and nobility, and reinforce the cause of human aspiration in its populace which has deteriorated into the "shadow of a people."

Mariano José de Larra, the nineteenth-century essayist, wrote penetrating diagnoses of Spanish ills and their possible remedies. Goytisolo acknowledges Larra's growing influence on post-Civil War generations, as he examines his life and times. Larra was interested in the social milieu in which he developed, in the realities of the moment which he hoped to change, and in the writer's responsibility to society. He encountered and fought censorship, employing literary devices to circumvent it, with an at times bitter but always keenly personal irony. Trying to establish a truly national and authentically popular culture, Larra, far from being the cynic critics have portrayed, was a man who saw in political struggle a possibility for practical morality, and in literature, faith in the progress of a people. Larra faced the problem confronting Goytisolo's generation, that of transforming society without modifying its characteristic "virtues."

Growing progressively more despondent, Larra committed suicide, a temptation, along with madness, against which Spanish intellectuals must struggle in their sometimes futile battle for a better Spain.

Censorship, based on Catholic morality and the interests of the State, controls anti-government writers through a complete critical silence in Spain about their literary creativity, or where necessary, through virulent newspaper attacks on their morality, honesty, or patriotism. Rehabilitated sinners, along with dead ones like Miguel Hernández or García Lorca, receive critical acclaim, but live ones like Goytisolo must await their inevitable death for official resurrection. The only practical result of the "liberalized" censorship is the release of the formerly withheld explanation of the reasons for rejection. These include literary justification of suicide, euthanasia, divorce, adultery, abortion, anti-Catholic principles, or statements against the State. The censorship itself has only stimulated writers to search for the necessary techniques to circumvent the censor in the presentation of their forbidden ideology.

Goytisolo examines the relationships between politics and literature in two literary generations. He defines the post-War generation as "that group of writers who began to publish after the end of hostilities and who were active protagonists or at least witnesses to that obscene and shameful episode of our ill-starred history . . ." [37] He considers them to be, with the notable exception of Camilo José Cela, traditional, conservative, and conformists, socially, morally, and religiously; he finds their language refined, anemic, and incapable of capturing or expressing the complexity of the modern world. His own "mid-century generation," on the contrary, is rebellious, leftist, agnostic, and vital. The writer involved in a fight for the transformation of man must have a double vision, both dramatic and ironic, of humanity and the world. He must strive for the fusion of personal experience, emotions, and ideas to achieve "necessary tension which will illuminate a new reality, not just a dead copy or simple prolongation of the emotions or ideas but an evident . . . truth for the one who communicates it and for the one who receives it . . ." [38] Only this tension and internal violence of experience can justify, in artistic terms, the need for transformation. The new world needs a new, anarchistic, and virulent language, for only by destroying antiquities can one create anew, as Latin American writers have discovered. Although Goytisolo admits that his own generation has not yet reached literary maturity, time yet remains for revision of past errors, rededication, and reevaluation.

He traces the development and the degeneration of the picaresque novel and its new view of reality. Of the many picaresque heroes, he finds Estebanillo González, protagonist of a seventeenth-century novel by the same name, the closest Spanish counterpart, in his cynicism and amorality, to the Genet portrayed in *Le journal du voleur* (Thief's Journal). Estebanillo, a skeptic and opportunist, applied the scalpel to himself without the philosophical or moral disgressions of the day; he tried to reform nothing, but humorously unrepentant, exposed an inverted mirror of society.

Goytisolo, who had previously discussed the literary criticism of Luis Cernuda, examines his poetic works, finding their leitmotif to be "opposition between the interior world of the artist and the contingent world, between reality and desire, contradiction which provokes in the poet a perpetual sentiment of estrangement and extirpation . . ." [39] Cernuda's antisocial and unconventional attitude regarding the laws and institutions held sacred by society evolved finally into an almost intransigent anarchism. *La realidad y el deseo* (Reality and Desire) sums up the bulk of his work written between 1924 and his death in 1963, revealing his attraction to contradictory viewpoints and his ambivalence toward life and death. His physical exile from Spain intensified and enriched his poetic, stylistic, and thematic content, purified his baroque tendencies, and turned his nostalgia into anger as he pessimistically despaired of cathartic or regenerative possibilities of Spain. His fellow poets, considering him too negative, consigned his poetry to a kind of limbo from which it has recently emerged to influence some of the best young poets of Spain. More than ever "his work appears alive to us . . . indispensable duty of those who did not understand it previously . . . to make it ours with a love identical to the one with which he elaborated it, before the scholar and the worms pounce voraciously and destroy it." [40]

Although Goytisolo admired Ramón Menéndez Pidal's contributions to Spanish culture and language, he attacks that great philologist and historian's manifest partiality and gratuitously willful reconstruction of Spanish history, regarding him as one of those responsible for the creation of a false Spain. Goytisolo examines Menéndez Pidal's studies on Father Bartolomé de las Casas, famous critic of the Spanish conquest of the New World. Menéndez Pidal, attacking Las Casas' doctrines as unreal, simplistic, antiquated, and medieval, expresses admiration instead for Francisco Vitoria's justification, on juridical, religious, and moral grounds, of the conquest, finding his ideas "modern and lasting." While Goytisolo admits the epic grandeur of the Spanish role in the new continent, he rejects Menéndez Pidal's biased and singularly obsessive viewpoint which denigrates those who see any defects in its participants or those who dare to criticize what the philologist regards with "imperialistic nostalgia."

Goytisolo, in spite of his critical and creative attacks on Spanish literary tradition, has inherited a number of classical techniques and has learned from Pío Baroja, Valle-Inclán, and many others. While he was the spokesman for his generation against the depersonalized values of Ortega y Gasset, he apparently accepted the latter's insistence on the value of artistic form, for in his generation, Goytisolo, the one most keenly aware of twentieth-century literary movements, is a constant experimenter with techniques such as interior monologue, stream of consciousness, objectivism (of sorts), flashbacks, other cinematographic techniques, and above all, temporal travel. If he has been one of the most outspoken critics of the Spanish government and the shrillest voice stressing the social purpose of contemporary literature and the responsibility of intellectuals, he has also espoused the vogue for technical and artistic form.

In all his novels, one may see, in addition to his attempts to present the truth hidden behind the veil of misrepresentation fostered by Spanish orthodoxy of the last quarter century, artistic as well as political integrity. He wants to shatter a closed archaic system while maintaining modern artistic insights. As one of the political and moral voices of the day, he fights against the fantasies and falsifications of the current scene. It is not surprising that his set of beliefs infused with passion has not received the critical acclaim in Spain that more acceptable beliefs have encountered. While he does not believe that the meek will inherit the earth nor that justice and virtue will triumph, he fights the good fight. Even though he is in a sense the most artistic writer of his generation (a fact denied by the defenders of Matute and Aldecoa), which may ensure his long-term survival, it is his refusal to accept authority in conflict with his moral code which makes him the leading Spanish novelist of his day.

Notes and References

Chapter One

1. Benjamin Welles, *Spain, The Gentle Anarchy* (New York, 1965), pp. 5-8.
2. *Ibid.*, p. 30.
3. *Ibid.*, p. 64.
4. Claude G. Bowers, *My Mission to Spain* (New York, 1954), p. 400.
5. *Ibid.*, pp. 376-77.
6. Welles, p. 122.
7. Juan Soto de Gangoiti, *Relaciones de la iglesia católica y el estado español (Relations of the Catholic Church and the Spanish State)* (Madrid, 1940), p. 11.
8. John Devlin, *Spanish Anticlericalism* (New York, 1966), pp. 202-5.
9. *Ibid.*, p. 205.
10. Hugh Thomas, *The Spanish Civil War* (New York, 1961), p. 211.

Chapter Two

1. Janet Winecoff, "The Contemporary Spanish Novel," *South Atlantic Modern Language Bulletin*, XXIX, no. 4 (1964), 1.
2. José María Castellet, "Juan Goytisolo y la novela española actual," *La Torre*, IX, no. 33 (1961), 132.
3. The Krausists based their theories on the German philosopher, Karl C. Krause (1781-1832), a disciple of Kant. They believed in tolerance, the scientific method, and the brotherhood of man. They were an important factor in the formation of the first Spanish Republic (1873-1874).
4. The Institute was founded in 1876 by Francisco Giner de los Ríos (1839-1915). He hoped to build a school free from partisan politics, based on beauty, tolerance, and love.
5. Ann Aikman, "Introducing Four First Novelists," *Mademoiselle*, XLVIII (1959), 85
6. *Ibid.*, 37.
7. José Corrales Egea, "Entrando en liza," *Insula*, nos. 152-53 (1959), 27.

8. Ramón Sender, "Fiestas," *Times Literary Supplement*, no. 2979 (April 3, 1959), pp. 185-86.

9. José R. Marra-López, *Ínsula*, XVII, no. 193 (1962), 4.

10. Castellet, 133.

11. Castellet, *Notas sobre literatura española contemporánea* (Barcelona, 1955), p. 89.

12. Letter to John B. Rust, July 2, 1954, as quoted by Maurice Coindreau in the Preface to *Jeux de Mains* (Paris: Gallimard, 1956), p. XIII.

13. Francisco Olmos García, "La novela y los novelistas españoles de hoy," *Cuadernos Americanos*, CXXIX (1963), 330.

14. *Ibid.*

15. E. P. Monroe, "Juan Goytisolo," *Saturday Review*, XLII (February 14, 1959), 28.

16. Castellet, "Veinte años de novela española," *Cuadernos Americanos*, CXXVI (1963), 290-95.

17. Domingo Pérez Minik, *Novelistas españoles de los siglos XIX y XX* (Madrid, 1957), pp. 334-35.

18. Letter to Maurice Coindreau, June 29, 1955, in *Jeux de Mains* (Paris, 1956), p. XX.

19. Juan Goytisolo, *Problemas de la novela* (Barcelona, 1959), p. 66.

20. Juan Goytisolo, "Formalismo o compromiso literario," *Casa de las Américas*, IV, no. 26 (1964), 149.

21. *Ibid.*, 152

22. Manuel Lamana, *Literatura de posguerra* (Buenos Aires, 1961), p. 36.

23. Janet Winecoff, 2.

24. D. L. Shaw, "A Reply to *Deshumanización*. Baroja on the Art of the Novel," *Hispanic Review*, XXV (1957), 105-11.

25. Pío Baroja, *La nave de los locos*, in *Obras completas* (Madrid, 1948), IV, 307-27.

26. Baroja, *Juventud, Egolatría* (Madrid, 1917), p. 54.

27. Fernando Baeza, *Baroja y su mundo* (Madrid, 1962), II, 72-87.

28. Goytisolo, *Ínsula*, no. 150 (1959), 11.

29. Goytisolo, "Para una literatura nacional popular," *Ínsula*, no. 146 (1959), pp. 6, 11.

30. Goytisolo, *Problemas de la novela*, p. 98.

31. Guillermo de Torre, "Los puntos sobre algunas íes novelísticas," *Ínsula*, XIV, no. 150 (1959), 1-2.

32. Guillermo de Torre, "Afirmación y negación de la novela española," *Ficción*, II (Buenos Aires, July-August, 1956), 122-41.

Notes and References

33. Castellet, "Coloquio internacional sobre novela en Formentor," *Cuadernos*, XXXVIII (Sept.-Oct., 1959), 86.

34. José Corrales Egea, "Entrando en liza," *Insula*, nos. 152-153 (1959), 26-27.

35. Jean Onimus, "L'Expression du Temps dans Le Roman Contemporain," *Revue de Littérature Comparée*, XXVIII (1954), 299-317.

36. Henri Bergson, *Time and Free Will* (New York, 1950), p. 104.

37. José Marra López, "Tres nuevos libros de Juan Goytisolo," *Insula*, XVII, no. 193 (1962), 4.

38. Eugenio de Nora, "La obra novelística de Juan Goytisolo," *Insula*, XVII, no. 190 (1962), 7.

39. José M. Martínez Cachero, "El novelista Juan Goytisolo," *Papeles de Son Armadans*, XXXII, no. 95 (1964), 160.

40. Ricardo Gullón, "The Modern Spanish Novel," *Texas Quarterly*, IV, no. 1 (1961), 86.

41. Gullón, "La novela española moderna," *La Torre*, XI, no. 42 (1963), 54-55.

42. Eugenio de Nora, *Insula*, no. 190, p. 7.

43. Paul West, "Leoquentia Standing Still: The Novel in Modern Spain," *Kenyon Review*, XXV, no. 2 (1963), 213-14.

44. José María Martínez Cachero, *Papeles*, XXXII, no. 95 (1964), 160.

45. Manuel de Lara, "Carta de Francia," *Papeles de Son Armadans*, XIV (1959), p. lv.

Chapter Three

1. Juan Goytisolo, *Juegos de manos* (Barcelona, 1960), p. 257.

2. *Ibid.*, pp. 41-42.

3. *La Torre*, IX, no. 33 (1961), 134.

4. José Luis Cano, "Juegos de Manos," *Insula*, no. 111 (March, 1955), 7.

5. Juan Goytisolo, *Fiestas*, tr. by Herbert Weinstock (New York, 1960), Jacket.

6. Castellet, *La Torre*, IX, no. 33 (1961), 136.

7. Cano, *Insula*, no 111 (1955), 7.

8. E. P. Monroe, *Saturday Review*, XLII (February 14, 1959), 28.

9. Castellet, *La Torre*, p. 135.

10. Goytisolo, *Juegos de manos*, pp. 10, 11, 13, 266.

11. Maurice Coindreau in Introduction to *Jeux de Mains* (Paris, 1956), p. xvii.

12. Goytisolo, *Juegos de manos*, pp. 87, 91.

13. *Ibid.*, pp. 92-93.
14. *Ibid.*, p. 97
15. *Ibid.*, p. 22.
16. *Ibid.*, p. 39.
17. *Ibid.*, pp. 142-43.
18. Robert Humphrey, *Stream of Consciousness in the Modern Novel* (Berkeley, California, 1965), p. 24.
19. Goytisolo, *Juegos de manos*, pp. 229-30.
20. Domingo Pérez Minik, *Novelistas españoles de los siglos xix y xx* (Madrid, 1957), p. 337.
21. Goytisolo, *Fiestas* (New York: 1960), Knopf, flyleaf.
22. *Ibid.*
23. *Ibid.*
24. David Dempsey, "The Young Assassins," *Saturday Review,* XLII (February 14, 1959), 28.
25. Ann Aikman, *Mademoiselle,* XLVIII (1959), 85.
26. Our comparison of the two novels was reached independently of the conclusions of Fernando Díaz Plaja, "Un paralelo narrativo, Goytisolo y Golding," *Insula,* no. 227 (Oct., 1965), 6.
27. Cano, *Insula,* no. 111 (1955), 7.
28. Jean Cocteau, *The Holy Terrors* (Norfolk, Connecticut, 1957), pp. 4-5.
29. Juan Goytisolo, *Duelo en el Paraíso* (Barcelona, 1960), pp. 188-89.
30. *Ibid.*, pp. 16-17.
31. *Ibid.*, pp. 155, 158.
32. *Ibid.*, p. 249.
33. José María Castellet, *La Torre,* 139.
34. Eugenio de Nora, *La novela española contemporánea* (Madrid, 1962), II, 320
35. *Duelo en el Paraíso,* p. 137.
36. *Ibid.*, p. 152.
37. *Ibid.*, p. 280.
38. Ibid., pp. 34-35.
39. *Ibid.*, p. 12.
40. *Ibid.*, p. 257.
41. *Ibid.*, p. 12.
42. José Luis Cano, "Con Juan Goytisolo en París," *Insula,* XII, no. 132 (1957), 8.
43. Goytisolo, *El circo* (Barcelona, 1957), p. 51.
44. *Ibid.*, p. 50.
45. Cano, "El circo," *Insula,* no. 136 (March, 1958), 15.
46. Goytisolo, *El circo,* p. 76.

Notes and References

47. *Ibid.*, p. 170.
48. Ramón María del Valle-Inclán, "Luces de Bohemia," in *Obras completas* (Madrid, 1952), pp. 938-39.
49. Goytisolo, *El circo*, p. 97.
50. *Ibid.*, p. 204.
51. Eugenio de Nora, *La novela española* (Madrid, 1962), p. 318.
52. Warren Eyster, "Two Spanish Novels," *Sewanee Review*, LXIX (1961), 700-704.
53. Ramón Sender, "Fiestas," *Saturday Review*, June 11, 1960, p. 35.
54. In a letter dated April 13, 1956. See *Jeux de Mains*, p. xxii.
55. *Fiestas* (Buenos Aires, 1958), p. 153.
56. *Fiestas* (New York, 1964), p. 217.
57. José Luis Cano, *Insula*, no. 132 (1957), 8.
58. *Fiestas* (Dell), p. 218.
59. José María Martínez Cachero, *Papeles*, XXXII (1965), 125-60.
60. *Ibid.*, p. 128.
61. José Francisco Cirre, "Novela e ideología en Juan Goytisolo," *Insula*, XXI, no. 230 (January, 1966), 12.
62. *Juegos de manos*, p. 146.
63. *El circo*, p. 46.
64. *Juegos de manos*, p. 142.
65. *Ibid.*, p. 162.
66. *Ibid.*, p. 99.
67. *Ibid.*, p. 253.
68. *Duelo en el Paraíso*, p. 231.
69. *Ibid.*, p. 286.
70. *El circo*, p. 244.
71. *Fiestas* (Emecé), p. 189.
72. Eugenio de Nora, *Insula*, no. 190 (1962), 7.

Chapter Four

1. F. Olmos García, *Cuadernos Americanos*, cxxix (1963), 230.
2. Goytisolo, *La resaca* (Paris, 1958), p. 275. Machado's poem, nevertheless, reflects the message Goytisolo hoped to convey.
3. *Ibid.*, p. 121.
4. *Ibid.*, p. 274
5. *Ibid.*, p. 61.
6. *Ibid.*, p. 146.
7. *Ibid.*, p. 79.
8. *Ibid.*, p. 93.
9. *Ibid.*, pp. 220-21.

10. *Ibid.*, p. 3.
11. *Ibid.*, pp. 22-26.
12. *Ibid.*, p. 65.
13. *Ibid.*, pp. 253-54.
14. *Ibid.*, p. 129.
15. Goytisolo, *La isla* (Barcelona, 1961), p. 14.
16. *Ibid.*, p. 11.
17. *Ibid.*, p. 124.
18. *Ibid.*, pp. 85-86.
19. Welles, *Spain, The Gentle Anarchy* (New York, 1965), p. 6.
20. Goytisolo, *La isla*, p. 132.
21. Eugenio de Nora, *La novela española*, p. 326.
22. Maurice Coindreau, in Juan Goytisolo, *Chronique d'une Ile*, tr. by Robert Marrast (Paris, 1961), p. 14.
23. Goytisolo, *Fin de fiesta* (Barcelona, 1962), p. 38.
24. *Ibid.*, p. 49.
25. *Ibid.*, p. 129.
26. *Ibid.*, pp. 187-88.
27. *Ibid.*, pp. 181-82.
28. Goytisolo, *Señas de identidad* (Mexico, 1966), p. 65.
29. *Ibid.*, pp. 376-77
30. *Ibid.*, p. 94
31. *Ibid.*, pp. 102-3
32. *Ibid.*, p. 64
33. *Ibid.*, pp. 57-58.
34. Virginia Woolf, *Orlando, a Biography* (London, 1942), p. 91.
35. Goytisolo, *Señas de identidad*, pp. 13-14.
36. *Ibid.*, pp. 27-35.
37. *Ibid,*, pp. 86-87.
38. *Ibid.*, pp. 40-41
39. *Ibid.*, p. 66.
40. *Ibid.*, p. 255.
41. *Ibid.*, p. 254
42. See *Mundo Nuevo,* 12 (1967), 44.
43. *Ibid.*, pp. 44-60.

Chapter Five

1. *Casa de las Américas,* Año II, nos. 11-12 (marzo-junio, 1962), 3-24.
2. See *Hudson Review,* XVI (1963), 61-67.
3. Goytisolo, *Para vivir aquí* (Buenos Aires, 1960), p. 17.
4. *Ibid.*, p. 116.
5. *Ibid.*, p. 121.

6. *Ibid.*, p. 171.
7. Celia Zaragoza, "Para vivir aquí," *Sur,* no. 269 (March-April, 1961), pp. 89-91.
8. *Ibid.*, p. 90.
9. Goytisolo, *Campos de Níjar* (Barcelona, 1960), p. 41.
10. *Ibid.*, p. 7.
11. *Ibid.*, p. 37
12. *Ibid.*, pp. 44-45.
13. José Ortega y Gasset, *The Dehumanization of Art and Other Writings on Art and Culture* (Garden City, New York, 1956), p. 95.
14. *Campos de Níjar,* pp. 68-69
15. Paul Werrie, "Le Cas de Juan Goytisolo," *La Table Ronde,* no. 204 (1965), 144.
16. *Campos de Níjar,* pp. 94-95.
17. *Ibid.*, p. 137.
18. Camilo José Cela, *Papeles de Son Armadans,* XXIII, no. 67 (1961), 7.
19. Camilo José Cela, *Mrs. Caldwell habla con su hijo* (Barcelona, 1958), p. 9
20. Camilo José Cela, *Tobogán de hambrientos* (Barcelona, 1962), pp. 16-17.
21. Cela, *Papeles de Son Armadans,* XXXIX, no. 117 (December, 1965), 227-34.
22. Paul Werrie, *La Table Ronde,* no. 204 (1965), 140.
23. Cleanth Brooks and Robert Penn Warren, *Understanding Fiction* (New York, 1959), p. 569.
24. Goytisolo, *La Chanca* (Paris, 1962), p. 9.
25. *Ibid.*, p. 40.
26. *Ibid.*, p. 120.
27. *Ibid.*, p. 130.
28. *Ibid.*, p. 140.
29. *Ibid.*, p. 178.
30. Goytisolo, *Pueblo en marcha* (Paris, 1963), p. 87.
31. *Ibid.*, p. 105.
32. *Ibid.*, p. 151.
33. Juan Goytisolo, *El furgón de cola* (Paris, Editions Ruedo Ibérico, 1967), p. 2.
34. *Ibid.*, p. 4.
35. *Ibid.*, p. 171.
36. *Ibid.*, p. 5
37. *Ibid.*, p. 47.
38. *Ibid.*, p. 53.
39. *Ibid.*, p. 102.
40. *Ibid.*, p. 114.

Selected Bibliography

Primary Sources

1. Works by Juan Goytisolo.
Juegos de manos (Barcelona: Destino, 1954).
Duelo en el Paraíso (Barcelona: Planeta, 1955).
El circo (Barcelona: Destino, 1957).
Fiestas (Buenos Aires: Editorial Emecé, 1958).
La resaca (Paris: Club del Libro Español, 1958).
Problemas de la novela (Barcelona: Editorial Seix Barral, 1959).
Campos de Níjar (Barcelona: Editorial Seix Barral, 1960).
Para vivir aquí (Buenos Aires: Editorial Sur, 1960).
La isla (Mexico: Editorial Seix Barral, 1961).
La chanca (Paris: Librería Española, 1962).
Fin de fiesta (Barcelona: Editorial Seix Barral, 1962).
Pueblo en marcha (Paris: Librería Española, 1963).
Fiestas (New York: Dell, 1964).
Señas de identidad (Mexico: Editorial Joaquín Mortiz, 1966).
El furgón de cola (Paris: Editions Ruedo Ibérico, 1967).

2. Translations.
Juegos de manos:
The Young Assassins. Tr. by John Rust (New York: Knopf, 1959).
Jeux de Mains. Tr. by Maurice Coindreau (Paris: Gallimard, 1956).
Duelo en el Paraíso:
Children of Chaos. Tr. by Christine Brooke-Rose (London: Mac-Gibbon and Kee, 1958).
Deuil au Paradis. Tr. by Maurice Coindreau (Paris: Gallimard, 1959).
Fiestas:
Fiestas. Tr. by Herbert Weinstock (New York: Knopf, 1960).
Para vivir aquí:
Pour vivre ici. Tr. by Bernard Lesfarques (Paris: Gallimard, 1962).
Campos de Níjar:
Terres de Nijar et La Chanca. Tr. by Robert Marrast (Paris: Gallimard, 1964)
La isla:
Island of Women. Tr. by José Yglesias (New York: Knopf, 1962).
Cronique d'une Île. Tr. by Robert Marrast (Paris: Gallimard, 1961).
Fin de fiesta:

Selected Bibliography

Danse d'été. Tr. by Maurice Coindreau (Paris: Gallimard, 1964).
The Party's Over. Tr. by José Yglesias (New York: Grove Press, 1966).

Secondary Sources

1. Books.
Alborg, Juan Luis. *Hora actual de la novela española* (Madrid: Taurus, 1958). Somewhat prejudiced but fairly good studies on various contemporary novelists.
Baeza, Fernando, *Baroja y su mundo* (Madrid: Ediciones Arlon, 1962, II). Contains much information on Baroja's style and technique.
Baroja, Pío. *Juventud, Egolatría* (Madrid: R. Caro Raggio, 1917). Discusses a variety of subjects, attacking religion as deceitful and stressing action as a cure for the evil of living.
———. *La nave de los locos. Obras completas* (Madrid: Biblioteca Nueva, 1948), IV, 307-27. A summary of his ideas on the "open novel" as a genre form.
Bergson, Henri. *Time and Free Will* (New York: Macmillan, 1950). The classical philosophical treatise on time.
Bowers, Claude G. *My Mission to Spain* (New York: Simon and Schuster, 1954). An excellent study of the events up to and including the Spanish Civil War. An admirably objective, though sympathetic account.
Brooks, Cleanth and Warren, Robert Penn. *Understanding Fiction* (New York: Appleton Century, 1959). A standard work by two well known critics, one of whom (Warren) is himself a novelist of stature.
Castellet, José María. *Notas sobre literatura española contemporánea* (Barcelona: Laye, 1955). Effective but limited information. These notes were never intended for a full treatment of the themes he discusses.
Cela, Camilo José. *Mrs. Caldwell habla con su hijo* 2nd ed. (Barcelona: Destino, 1958). An excellent statement in the prologue about his ideas on the novel.
———. *Tobogán de hambrientos* (Barcelona: Ed. Noguer, 1962). Further elaboration in the prologue of the author's ideas on widening the definition of the novel.
Cocteau, Jean. *The Holy Terrors* (Norfolk, Connecticut: New Directions, 1957). A fictional study of juvenile loves and delinquency.
Devlin, John. *Spanish Anticlericalism* (New York: Las Americas Publishing Co., 1966). A plea for the spirit of ecumenism in an examination of modern Spanish authors' viewpoints.

Hoyos, Antonio de. *Ocho escritores actuales* (Murcia: Aula de Cultura, 1954). Adds new facts about the contemporary novel, although not about Goytisolo.

Humphrey, Robert. *Stream of Consciousness in the Modern Novel* (Berkeley: University of California Press, 1965). An excellent study of this and similar techniques used in the twentieth century.

Lamana, Manuel. *Literatura de posguerra* (Buenos Aires: Ed. Nova, 1961). Full of generalizations but interesting for its comparison of French and Spanish literature.

Nora, Eugenio de. *La novela española contemporánea* (Madrid: Ed. Gredos, 1962, II). The most complete study of the twentieth-century Spanish novel. Extensive but somewhat biased information on Juan Goytisolo.

Ortega y Gasset, José. *The Dehumanization of Art and Other Writings on Art and Culture* (New York: Doubleday, 1956). Basic to an understanding of the polemics on literature and the novel of the twentieth century. Goytisolo both uses and attacks Ortega's ideas.

Pérez Minik, Domingo. *Novelistas españoles de los siglos xix y xx* (Madrid: Ediciones Guadarrama, 1957). Better on the twentieth century than on the nineteenth. Compares Spanish novels with those of other countries.

Sáinz de Robles, Federico C. *La novela española en el siglo xx* (Madrid: Pegaso, 1957). Wordy and superficial but contains many facts.

Soto de Gangoiti, Juan. *Relaciones de la iglesia católica y el estado español* (Madrid: Instituto Editorial Reus, 1940). Explores the relationship between the Catholic Church and Spanish law up to 1931 and again from July 18, 1936 on.

Thomas, Hugh. *The Spanish Civil War* (New York: Harper, 1961). Undoubtedly one of the best documented accounts of that conflict.

Torrente Ballester, Gonzalo. *Panorama de la literatura española contemporánea* (Madrid: Ed. Guadarrama, 1956). One of the standard works on contemporary Spanish literature.

Valle-Inclán, Ramón María del. *Luces de Bohemia. Obras completas* (Madrid: Plenitud, 1952). A famous esperpento drama and early example of the theater of the absurd.

Welles, Benjamin. *Spain, The Gentle Anarchy* (New York: Frederick Praeger, 1965). An excellent study of the political, religious, and social forces in Spain in the last twenty-five years.

Woolf, Virginia. *Orlando, a Biography* (London: The Hogarth Press,

1942). Interesting for its contribution to temporal and other modern techniques in literature.

2. Articles.

Aikman, Ann. "Introducing Four First Novelists," *Mademoiselle*, XLVIII (January, 1959), 37, 85. Contains some intimate biographical details on Goytisolo.

Albérès, R. M. "La Renaissance du Roman Espagnol," *Revue de Paris*, (Oct., 1961), pp. 81-91. A sketchy summary of some of the new forces at work. Albérès examines the crude reality and finds neorealism a remarkable phenomenon.

Azcoaga, Enrique. "Juan Goytisolo y los problemas de la novela," *Ficción*, no. 27 (Sept.-Oct., 1960), 95-98. Disagrees with Goytisolos' *Problemas de la novela* and stresses the need for a theory of the novel which will humanize life

Bosch, Rafael. "The Style of the New Spanish Novel," *Books Abroad*, XXXIX (1965), 10-14. Discusses types of the new novel and examines especially the reportorial, documentary novels which he finds basically realistic and social.

Cano, José Luis. "El circo," *Insula*, no. 136 (March, 1958), 6. Examines symbolic values of the protagonist, Utah, viewing the novel as a social satire and not as a farce.

———. "Duelo en el Paraíso," *Insula*, no. 118 (October, 1955), 6. Recognizes Goytisolo's undeniable narrative talent and the cinematic and poetic qualities of the work.

———. "Juegos de manos," *Insula*, no. 111 (March, 1955), 7. In times of crisis young authors can live intensely. Cano sees antecedents of the novel in Gide's *Les faux-monnayeurs* and in Cocteau's *Les enfants terribles*.

Castellet, José María. Introduction to *Deuil au Paradis* (Paris: Gallimard, 1959), pp. 7-18. Stresses the social preoccupations and interest in children of the generation of 1950.

———. "La joven novela española," *Sur*, no. 284 (1963), 48-54. Examines difference in themes and motivation of two post-Civil War generations, especially the "witness" novels after the political disturbances of 1956.

———. "Juan Goytisolo y la novela española actual," *La Torre*, IX, no. 33 (1961), 131-40. Finds the authentic *Duelo* better than the unrealistic *Juegos*.

———. "Veinte años de novela española (1942-1962)," *Cuadernos Americanos*, XXII, cxxvi (1963), 290-95. With *Pascual Duarte* as departure point, discusses historical realism and its hope for the future.

Cela, Camilo José. "Dos tendencias de la nueva literatura española,"

Papeles de Son Armadans, XXVII, no. 79 (1962), 3-20. Examines so-called tremendism and objectivism and the importance of literary tradition.

Cirre, José Francisco. "El protagonista múltiple y su papel en la novela española," *Papeles de Son Armadans,* XXXIII (1964), 159-70. Many protagonists in one novel share problems in common in novels such as Cela's *La colmena.* Man's anguish is non-existential, and in the Spanish novel is the anguish of a man who cannot find himself as a man.

———. "Novela e ideología en Juan Goytisolo," *Insula,* XXI, no. 230 (Jan., 1966), 1, 12. Examines internal contradictions of Goytisolo's novels in their poetic view of life through the photographic eye, and the need for the limitation of political themes in his novels.

Coindreau, Maurice E. "Homenaje a los jóvenes novelistas españoles," *Cuadernos,* no. 33 (Nov.-Dec., 1958), 44-47. Discusses Goytisolo's breaching of foreign opposition to the Spanish novel, his international contacts, and compares his adolescents to those of Ana María Matute.

———. Introduction to *Cronique d'une Ile* (Paris: Gallimard, 1961), pp. 7-14. Sees new development in Goytisolo, examines artistic merit of *La isla.*

———. Introduction to *Jeux de Mains* (Paris: Gallimard, 1956), pp. 9-24. Examines development of new generation of novelists with Cela, Juan Goytisolo's letter to John Rust about literary influences, and briefly comments on *Fiestas* and *Juegos de manos.*

Corrales Egea, José. "Entrando en liza," *Insula,* nos. 152-153 (July-August, 1959), 26-27. An ardent defense of Goytisolo's theories of the novel as opposed to those of Guillermo de Torre.

Couffon, Claude. "Las tendencias de la novela española actual," *Revista Nacional de Cultura,* XXIV, cliv (1962), 15-27. Discusses origins of the new novel from Cela on, and the role of the adolescent and man in the new novel.

Dempsey, David. "The Young Assassins," *Saturday Review,* XLII (Feb. 14, 1959), 28. Sees the work as beginning where Kerouac's work leaves off.

Destino, no. 857 (Sept. 1, 1954), 16-17. Important as the first reference to *Juegos de manos* in an anonymous review article.

Díaz Plaja, Fernando. "Un paralelo narrativo, Goytisolo y Golding," *Insula,* no. 227 (Oct., 1965), 6. Compares *Lord of the Flies* and *Duelo en el Paraíso.*

Eyster, Warren. "Two Spanish Novels," *Sewanee Review,* LXIX (1961), 700-704. Finds Goytisolo's novels juvenile and badly written. Considers *Fiestas* especially poor.

Selected Bibliography

Ferguson, Albert G. "Spain Through Her Novel, 1940-1960," *Dissertation Abstracts*, XXIV (1963), 1615 (Neb.). Studies changes in mores and attitudes in the contemporary novel and sees hopeful signs of new awareness and precepts of Christianity on the part of younger priests.

Ferrer, Olga P. "La literatura española tremendista y su nexo en el existencialismo," *Revista Hispánica Moderna*, XXII (1965), 297-303. Examines the relationship of existentialism to tremendism in various novels from Cela's on and views tremendism as a definite aspect of Spanish existentialism.

Fornet, Ambrosio. "La isla," *Casa de las Américas*, II (Nov., 1962-Feb., 1963), 52-55. Examines social implications of the work and analyses characters.

Goytisolo, Juan. "Formalismo o compromiso literario," *Casa de las Américas*, IV, no. 26 (Oct.-Nov., 1964), 148-52. Stresses the need for the novelist to be involved in political causes, especially in Spain. He comments on the situation in France and on Robbe-Grillet's theories.

————. "Para una literatura nacional popular," *Insula*, no. 146 (Jan. 15, 1959), 6, 11. The Spanish novel must become truly popular as it reflects meaningful contemporary problems, but popular does not mean vulgar.

Gullón, Ricardo. "The Modern Spanish Novel," *Texas Quarterly*, IV, no. 1 (1961). This same article later appeared in Spanish in *La Torre*. See below.

————. "La novela española moderna," *La Torre*, XI, no. 42 (1963), 45-68. The modern novel begins with Galdós. Goytisolo is not representative of the contemporary novel. The two best novelists are probably Cela and Ayala.

Hornedo, Rafael. "La novela española contemporánea," *Razón y Fe*, CLX (1959), 419-31. Discusses the trends from Cela on.

Mallo, Jerónimo. "Caracterización y valor del 'tremendismo' en la novela española contemporánea," *Hispania*, XXXIX (1956), 49-55. Defines tremendism and examines variants in the works of Cela, Laforet, and Sebastián Juan Arbó.

Marra-López, José R. "Tres nuevos libros de Juan Goytisolo," *Insula*, XVII, no. 193 (1962), 4. Examines *La Chanca*, *La isla*, and *Fin de fiesta*. Sees *La Chanca* as a travel book and complains that Goytisolo examines only one segment of the rich classes in *La isla*. In general laments Goytisolo's limited novelistic world.

Martínez-Cachero, José María. "El novelista Juan Goytisolo," *Papeles de Son Armadans*, XXXII, no. 95 (1964), 125-60. Examines literary beginnings, the uniqueness of *Duelo en el Paraíso*, analyses the author's technique, divides his work into three periods, and laments the growing incorrectness of Goytisolo's language.

Monroe, E. P. "Juan Goytisolo," *Saturday Review*, XLII (Feb. 14, 1959), 28. An autobiographical note.

Nora, Eugenio de. "La obra novelística de Juan Goytisolo," *Insula*, XVII, no. 190 (1962), 7. Sees as special factors Goytisolo's youthful beginnings, his Catalan-Basque origin, and examines recurring themes and types in his novels. Feels his novelistic force is undermined by grave defects. Views him as a novelist in formation whose experiences have not caught up to his ideas.

Olmos García, Francisco. "La novela y los novelistas españoles de hoy," *Cuadernos Americanos*, XXII, cxxix (1963), 211-27. Examines the social service of the new novelists from Cela on, commenting, author by author, on the origin of their works and giving brief biographical data.

Onimus, Jean. "L'Expression du Temps dans le Roman Contemporain," *Revue de Littérature Comparée*, XXVIII (1954), 299-317. Examines temporal excursions in the novel and how this has affected structure in the novel.

Ornstein, J., and Causey, J. "Una década de la novela española contemporánea," *Revista Hispánica Moderna*, XVII (1951), 128-35. Examines works of Benítez de Castro, Juan Antonio de Zunzunegui, Camilo José Cela, along with a few others, and sees a continuing realism for the novel.

Palley, Julián. "Existentialist Trends in the Modern Spanish Novel," *Hispania*, XLIV (1961), 21-26. Examines existential themes in novelists such as Sender, Quiroga, and Goytisolo, and wonders if existentialism has spent itself as a basis for literary expression.

Pragg Chantraine, J. Van. "El pícaro en la novela española moderna," *Revista Hispánica Moderna*, XXIX (1963), 223-31. Examines the *pícaro's* persistence in Spanish literature and the greater psychology and humanity of modern picaresque types.

Robbe-Grillet, Alain. "Le Nouveau Roman," *La Revue de Paris* (Sept., 1961), pp. 115-21. The author gives his basic tenets about the objectivist novel, the need for the reality of the here and now, and the disengagement of the author from the painted reality.

Schwartz, Kessel. Introduction to *Fiestas* (New York: Dell, 1964), pp. 7-24. An overall summary of Goytisolo's life and works.

———. "The Novels of Juan Goytisolo," *Hispania*, XLVII (May, 1964), 302-8. Contains plot summaries and critical commentary on Goytisolo's works.

Selected Bibliography

————. "The United States in the Novels of Juan Goytisolo," *Romance Notes*, VI, no. 2 (1965), 122-25.

Sender, Ramón. "Fiestas," *Saturday Review* (June 11, 1960), 35. Claims that *Fiestas* is harmonious, brilliant and original.

————. "Fiestas," *Times Literary Supplement*, no. 2979 (April 3, 1959), 185-86. Views Goytisolo as the best writer of his generation.

Shaw, D. L. "A Reply to *Deshumanización;* Baroja on the Art of the Novel," *Hispanic Review*, XXV (April, 1957), 105-11. An examination of the famous polemic between Ortega and Baroja and the latter's view of the novel.

Torre, Guillermo de. "Afirmación y negación de la novela española," *Ficción*, II (July-August, 1956), 122-41. Shows the unique capacity of Spanish novelists to express this dualism.

——. "Los puntos sobre algunas íes novelísticas," *Insula*, XIV, no. 150 (May 15, 1959), 1-2. Replies to Goytisolo's manifesto of January, 1959; says his arguments on popularism, naturalism, and realism are weak, repeats Ortega's concept of stylizing and deforming, and accuses Goytisolo of publicity seeking for the sake of publication.

Torrente Ballester, Gonzalo. "Los problemas de la novela española contemporánea," *Arbor*, IX (1948), 395-400. Views the novel (up to 1948) as in a period of crisis. The novelists, lacking national traditions, take refuge in stylistic devices, as they follow their disparate paths. Sees the need for a universal realism.

Werrie, Paul. "Le cas de Juan Goytisolo," *La Table Ronde*, no. 204 (1965), 141-47. A negative view of *Campos de Níjar* and *La Chanca* as novels. Views Goytisolo's translations into French as of uneven merit.

West, Paul. "Leoquentia Standing Still. The Novel in Modern Spain," *Kenyon Review*, XXV (1963), 203-16. Discusses the debt owed by the modern novel to Baroja and Valle-Inclán, and after commenting on novelists such as Sender, Cela, and Goytisolo, compares the new novel to non-representational art.

Winecoff, Janet. "The Contemporary Spanish Novel," *South Atlantic Bulletin*, XXIX, 4 (Nov., 1964), 1-4. Mentions Goytisolo as an objectivist novelist who has tried for a certain notoriety. Discusses the great variety among Spanish novelists, and their motivations.

Zaragoza, Celia. "Para vivir aquí," *Sur*, no. 269 (March-April, 1961), pp. 89-91. Sees anti-Franco overtones in Goytisolo's short stories.

Additional Recent Secondary Sources

1. Books.

Buckley, Ramón. *Problemas formales en la novela contemporánea* (Barcelona: Ediciones Península, 1968).

Curutchet, Juan Carlos. *Introducción a la novela española de posguerra* (Montevideo, 1966).

2. Articles.

Domingo, José. "La última novela de Goytisolo," *Insula*, XXII (July-August, 1967), 13.

Garasa, Delfín L. "La condición humana en la narrativa española contemporánea," *Atenea*, XLIII, 162 (1966), 109-38.

Gil Casado, Pablo P. "La novela social en España," *Cuadernos Americanos*, 154, (1967), 230-36.

Gómez Marín, José Antonio. "Literatura y política del tremendismo a la nueva narrativa," *Cuadernos Hispanoamericanos*, LXV (1966), 109-16.

Goytisolo, Juan. "Destrucción de la España Sagrada," *Mundo Nuevo*, 12 (1967), 44-60.

Peden, Margaret. "Juan Goytisolo's *Fiestas*—Analysis and Commentary," *Hispania*, L (1967), 461-66.

Sobejano, Gonzalo. "Notas sobre lenguaje y novela actual," *Papeles de Son Armadans*, XL (1966), 125-40.

Soldevila-Durante, Ignacio. "La novela española actual," *Revista Hispánica Moderna*, XXXIII (1967), 89-108.

Index

[154]

Index